# A VISUAL HISTORY OF COSTUME The Fourteenth & Fifteenth Centuries

## MARGARET SCOTT

# Acknowledgements

Published in Great Britain by
B. T. Batsford Ltd
4 Fitzhardinge Street
London W1H 0AH

ISBN 0 7134 4857 1

Typeset by
Keyspools Ltd
Golborne, Lancashire
and printed in Great Britain
by Anchor Brendon Ltd
Tiptree, Essex

My thanks go to the staff of many libraries and insti-
tutions, particularly of the National Monuments Record,
the Witt Library at the Courtauld Institute of Art, the
Photographic Library at the Victoria and Albert Museum,
and the Typewriter Department at Selfridges. My parents
must also be thanked for accepting, without protest, that
the completion of this book would require that I abandon
my habit of spending Easter with them.

Those who kindly gave their permission for the
reproduction of works whose copyright they own are
acknowledged in the List of Illustrations.

Last but not least, my gratitude to Dr Aileen Ribeiro for
persuading me to write this book, and to Tim Auger of
Batsford for soothing my moments of panic.

# Contents

# Preface

*A Visual History of Costume* is a series devised for those who need reliable, easy-to-use reference material on the history of dress.

The central part of each book is a series of illustrations, in black-and-white and colour, taken from the time of the dress itself. They include oil paintings, engravings, woodcuts and line drawings. By the use of such material, the reader is given a clear idea of what was worn and how, without the distortions and loss of detail which modern drawings can occasionally entail.

Each picture is captioned in a consistent way, under the headings, where appropriate, 'Head', 'Body' and 'Accessories'; the clothes are not just described, but their significance explained. The reader will want to know whether a certain style was fashionable or unfashionable at a certain time, usual or unusual – such information is clearly and consistently laid out. The illustrations are arranged in date order, and the colour illustrations are numbered in sequence with the black-and-white, so that the processes of change can be clearly followed.

The pictures will be all the better appreciated if the reader has at least some basic overall impression of the broad developments in dress in the period concerned, and the Introduction is intended to provide this.

Technical terms have been kept to a reasonable minimum. Many readers will use these books for reference, rather than read them straight through from beginning to end. To explain every term every time it is used would have been hopelessly repetitive, and so a Glossary has been provided. Since the basic items of dress recur throughout the book, a conventional, full Index would have been equally repetitive, therefore the Glossary has been designed also to act as an Index; after each entry the reader will find the numbers of those illustrations which show important examples of the item concerned.

# List of Illustrations

**Note** The subject is followed by the artist, where known (attrib. = attributed), the medium or nature of the artefact, the location or collection, and, if different, the owner of the copyright of the illustration. The colour plates, marked thus *, are between pp. 96 and 97. RCHME = Royal Commission on Historical Monuments (England).

17  **Blanche Mortimer, Lady Grandison**
Anon. English sculptor
Freestone effigy
Church of St Bartholomew, Much Marcle,
Herefordshire
RCHME

18  **Prince William of Hatfield(?)**
Anon. English sculptor
Alabaster effigy
Minster, York
Courtauld Institute

19  **An unidentified member of the Cockayne(?)
family**
Anon. English sculptor
Freestone effigy
Church of St Oswald, Ashbourne, Derbyshire
RCHME

20  **Guillaume de Machaut sings as his lady
dances**
Anon. French illuminator
*Le Remède de fortune*, MS fr. 1586, f. 51
Bibliothèque Nationale, Paris

21  **Robert Braunche, merchant of King's Lynn,
and his wives Letice and Margaret**
Anon. Flemish engraver
Brass rubbing
Church of St Margaret, King's Lynn, Norfolk
Victoria and Albert Museum, Crown Copyright

22  **Two unknown men**
Anon. English sculptor
Freestone effigies
Abbey, Shrewsbury (from Church of St Alkmund)
Courtauld Institute

23  **Walter Helyon**
Anon. English sculptor
Oak effigy
Church of St Bartholomew, Much Marcle,
Herefordshire
Batsford

24  **An unknown man**
Anon. English engraver
Brass rubbing
Church of St Thomas Becket, Hampsthwaite,
Yorks.
Victoria and Albert Museum, Crown Copyright

25  **A lady, said to be the wife of Sir John Jose of
Clearwell**
Anon. English sculptor
Freestone effigy
Church of All Saints, Newland, Gloucs.
RCHME

26  **Queen Philippa of Hainault, wife of Edward III**
Hennequin of Liège
Marble effigy
Westminster Abbey, London
RCHME

27  **Jean de Vaudetar presenting the *Bible
Historiale* to Charles V of France**
John of Bruges
*Bible Historiale*, MS 10 B 23, f. 2
Museum Meermanno-Westreenianum, The Hague

28  **Catherine, Countess of Warwick**
Anon. English sculptor
Alabaster effigy
Church of St Mary, Warwick
Canon Ridgway

29  **Sir Godferey Foljambe and his wife Avena**
Anon. English sculptor
Alabaster effigies
Church of All Saints, Bakewell, Derbyshire
RCHME

30  **A wedding**
The *Parement* master
*The Hours of Milan*, f. 87
Museo Civico, Turin

31  **Joan de Cobham, wife of Sir John de la Pole**
Anon. English engraver
Brass rubbing
Church of the Holy Trinity, Chrishall, Essex
Victoria and Albert Museum, Crown Copyright

32  **The two wives of Sir Reynald de Malyns**
Anon. English engraver
Brass rubbing
Church of St Andrew, Chinnor, Oxon.
Victoria and Albert Museum, Crown Copyright

33  **Female weeper from the tomb of Edward III**
John Orchard(?)
Gilt-bronze figurine
Westminster Abbey, London
A.F.Kersting

34  **Male weeper from the tomb of Edward III**
John Orchard(?)
Gilt-bronze figurine
Westminster Abbey, London
A.F.Kersting

35  **William Grevel, wool merchant, and his wife
Marion**
Anon. English engraver
Brass
Church of St James, Chipping Campden, Glos.
RCHME

36 **Hantascia Disney**
Anon. English sculptor
Freestone effigy
Church of St Peter, Norton Disney, Lincs.
RCHME

37 **Sir John Cassy, Chief Baron of the Exchequer, and his wife Alice Giffard**
Anon. English engraver
Brass rubbing
Church of St Mary, Deerhurst, Glos.
RCHME

38* **Richard II with St Edmund, Edward the Confessor and John the Baptist, from 'The Wilton Diptych'**
Anon. French(?) painter
Tempera on panel
The National Gallery, London

39 **Angels wearing the livery badges of Richard II, from 'The Wilton Diptych'**
Anon. French(?) painter
Tempera on panel
The National Gallery, London

40 **The monk Philippe de Maizieres presenting a book to Richard II**
Anon. French illuminator
Royal MS 20 B V, f. 2
The British Library, London

41 **An unknown civilian and his wife**
Anon. English engraver
Brass rubbing
Church of All Saints, Tilbrook, Huntingdonshire
Victoria and Albert Museum, Crown Copyright

42 **John de Oteswich and his wife Mary**
Anon. English sculptor
Alabaster effigies
Church of St Helen, Bishopsgate, City of London
RCHME

43 **Edward Courtenay(?)**
Anon. English sculptor
Alabaster effigy
Church of St Blaise, Haccombe, Devon
RCHME

44 **Lady Arderne**
Anon. English sculptor
Alabaster effigy
Church of St Peter, Elford, Staffs.
Canon Ridgway

45* **Chaucer reciting before an elegant audience**
Anon. English illuminator
Chaucer, *Troilus and Criseyde*, MS 61, f. 1v
The Master and Fellows of Corpus Christi College, Cambridge

46 **The Sun**
Anon. English illuminator
John Foxton, *Liver Cosmographiae*, MS R 15.21 (943), f. 35v
The Master and Fellows of Trinity College, Cambridge

47 **John Gower, the poet**
Anon. English sculptor
Freestone(?) effigy
Southwark Cathedral, London
RCHME

48 **An unknown lady**
Anon. English sculptor
Freestone effigy
Church of St Bartholomew, Much Marcle, Herefordshire
RCHME

49 **Lady Elizabeth Blackett, wife of Sir William Wilcote**
Anon. English sculptor
Alabaster effigy
Church of St Mary, North Leigh, near Oxford
Canon Ridgway

50 **One of the wives of Ralph Nevill, first Earl of Westmorland: Margaret Stafford or Joan Beaufort**
Anon. English sculptor
Alabaster effigy
Church of St Mary, Staindrop, County Durham
RCHME

51 **Lady Mainwaring**
Anon. English sculptor
Alabaster effigy
Church of St Lawrence, Over Peover, Cheshire
Canon Ridgway

52 **Clarice, wife of Robert de Frevile**
Anon. English engraver
Brass rubbing
Church of All Saints, Little Shelford, Cambs.
Victoria and Albert Museum, Crown Copyright

53 **John Urban and his wife Joan Reskymmer**
Anon. English engraver
Brass rubbing
Church of St Nicholas, Southfleet, Kent
Victoria and Albert Museum, Crown Copyright

54 **Lucy, wife of William, Baron Willoughby d'Eresby, and daughter of Roger, Lord Strange of Knokyn**
Anon. English engraver
Brass rubbing
Church of St James, Spilsby, Lincs.
Victoria and Albert Museum, Crown Copyright

55 **Brother Jean Hayton presenting the *Livre des merveilles du monde* to John the Fearless, Duke of Burgundy**
Anon. French illuminator
*Livre des merveilles du monde*, ms fr. 2810, f. 226
Bibliothèque Nationale, Paris

56 **Louis II of Anjou**
Anon. French painter
Watercolour on paper
Cabinet des Estampes, Bibliothèque Nationale, Paris

57 **A lady with a falcon and a lapdog**
Anon. Netherlandish painter
Watercolour and gouache on vellum
Cabinet des dessins, Musée du Louvre, Paris
Musées Nationaux

58 **Joan Risain, wife of John Peryent**
Anon. English engraver
Brass rubbing
Church of St John the Evangelist, Digswell, Herts.
Victoria and Albert Museum, Crown Copyright

59 **Katherine, widow of Ralph Greene**
Thomas Prentys and Robert Sutton of Chellaston
Alabaster effigy
Church of St Peter, Lowick, Northants.
Canon Ridgway

60 **Beatrix, Countess of Arundel**
Anon. English sculptor
Alabaster effigy
Church of St Nicholas, Arundel, Sussex
Canon Ridgway

61 **Millicent Bekeryng, wife of Sir William Meryng**
Anon. English engraver
Brass
Church of John the Baptist, East Markham, Notts.
A.F.Kersting

62 **Sir William Gascoigne, Lord Chief Justice, and his wife Elizabeth Mowbray**
Anon. English sculptor
Alabaster effigies
Church of All Saints, Harewood, Yorks.
Professor Lawrence Stone

63 **A lady receives a suitor**
Anon. French illuminator
*Poems of Christine de Pisan*, Harley MS. 4431, f. 56v
The British Library, London

64 **Two male weepers from the tomb of Lady Clinton**
Anon. English sculptor
Alabaster figurines
Church of St Mary, Haversham, Bucks.
RCHME

65 **Duke John IV of Brabant**
Anon. Flemish draughtsman
Silverpoint drawing
Museum Boymans-van Beuningen, Rotterdam

66 **A fishing party at the court of Holland**
Anon. Dutch or Flemish draughtsman
Watercolour with highlights of gold and white gouache
Cabinet des dessins, Musée du Louvre, Paris
Musées Nationaux

67 **Wenllan Walsche, wife of W. Moreton**
Anon. English(?) engraver
Brass rubbing
Church of St Dôchdwy, Llandough, Glamorgan
Victoria and Albert Museum, Crown Copyright

68 **An unknown man**
Robert Campin (attrib.)
Oil on panel
The National Gallery, London

69 **An unknown woman**
Robert Campin (attrib.)
Oil on panel
The National Gallery, London

70 **Catherine of Cleves distributing alms**
Northern Netherlandish illuminator
The Hours of Catherine of Cleves, M. 917, p. 65
The Pierpoint Morgan Library, New York

71 **A lady playing a portable organ**
Northern Netherlandish draughtsman
Pen and ink drawing
Cabinet des dessins, Musée du Louvre, Paris
Musées Nationaux

72 **'Leal Souvenir'**
Jan van Eyck
Oil on panel
The National Gallery, London

73 **A man in a turban**
Jan van Eyck
Oil on panel
The National Gallery, London

74* **The marriage of Giovanni Arnolfini and Giovanna Cenami**
Jan van Eyck
Oil on panel
The National Gallery, London

75 **William Welley, merchant, and his wife Alicia**
Anon. English engraver
Brass rubbing
Church of St James, Chipping Campden, Glos.
RCHME

94 **Flemish street scene, with presentaion of a book to Philip the Good of Burgundy in the background**
Jean le Tavernier
*Conquestes de Charlemagne*, MS 9066, f. 11
Bibliothèque Royale, Brussels

95 **Philip the Good, Duke of Burgundy, and the Duchess, Isabella of Portugal, at prayer with their courtiers**
Anon. Flemish illuminator
*Breviary of Philip the Good*, MS 9026, f. 258
Bibliothèque Royale, Brussels

96* **An unknown young woman**
Rogier van der Weyden (studio of)
Oil on panel
The National Gallery, London

97 **Joan, wife of William Canynge, merchant and mayor of Bristol**
Anon. English sculptor
Freestone effigy
Church of St Mary Redcliff, Bristol
Batsford

98 **William Canynge, husband of Joan Canynge**
Anon. English sculptor
Freestone effigy
Church of St Mary Redcliff, Bristol
Batsford

99 **Heinrich Blarer**
Anon. South German artist
Oil on panel
Rosgarten Museum, Konstanz

100 **An unknown man**
Dirk Bouts
Oil on panel
The National Gallery, London

101 **Barbara Vetzer and her daughter (detail)**
Friedrich Walther
Oil on panel
Historisches Museum, Bern

102 **Bertha, Duchess of Burgundy, supervising the building of the church of the Magdalene, Vezelay**
Loyset Liédet
*L'histoire de Charles Martel*, ms 6, f. 554v
Bibliothèque Royale, Brussels

103 **Gerard de Roussillon and his wife Berthe are presented by the Queen of France to Charles the Bald**
Loyset Liédet
*L'histoire de Charles Martel*, ms 7, f. 27v
Bibliothèque Royale, Brussels

104 **William Gybbys and his wives Alice, Margaret and Marion**
Anon. English engraver
Brass rubbing
Church of St James, Chipping Campden, Glos.
RCHME

105 **A woman of the Hofer family**
Swabian school
Oil on panel
The National Gallery, London

106 **An older woman**
Hans Memlinc
Oil on panel
Musée du Louvre, Paris
Musées Nationaux

107 **Sir John Curzon and his wife Joan**
Anon. English engraver
Brass rubbing
Church of St Mary, Bylaugh, Norfolk
Batsford

108 **Robert Ingylton and his wives Margaret Dymoke, Clemens Cantilupe and Isabel Lester, and their children**
Anon. English engraver
Brass rubbing
Church of St Michael, Thornton, Bucks.
Victoria and Albert Museum, Crown Copyright

109 **Jan de Witte, aged 30**
Bruges Master of 1473
Oil on panel
Musées Royaux des Beaux-Arts, Brussels
ACL, Brussels

110 **Maria Hoose, aged 17**
Bruges Master of 1473
Oil on panel
Musées Royaux des Beaux-Arts, Brussels
ACL, Brussels

111 **Margaret of Denmark, Queen of James III of Scotland, with St George**
Hugo van der Goes
Oil on panel
The National Gallery of Scotland, Edinburgh, on loan from H.M. The Queen
By gracious permission of H.M. The Queen

112 **Sophia von Bylant with St James the Greater**
The Master of the St Bartholomew Altarpiece
*The Book of Hours of Sophia von Bylant*
Wallraf-Richartz Museum, Cologne
Rheinisches Bildarchiv

113 **An unknown young man at prayer**
Hans Memlinc
Oil on panel
The National Gallery, London

10

114* **Sir John Donne (detail from 'The Donne Triptych')**
Hans Memlinc
Oil on panel
The National Gallery, London

115* **Lady Donne and her daughter (detail from 'The Donne Triptych')**
Hans Memlinc
Oil on panel
The National Gallery, London

116 **One of the two wives of (?)John Carent of Silton**
Anon. English sculptor
Alabaster effigy
Church of St Gregory, Marnhull, Dorset
RCHME

117 **The widow and family of Sir Thomas Urswyck, Recorder of London and Chief Baron of the Exchequer**
Anon. English engraver
Brass rubbing
Church of St Peter and St Paul, Dagenham, Essex
Victoria and Albert Museum, Crown Copyright

118 **An unknown lady, sometimes called Alice Neville**
Anon. English sculptor
Alabaster effigy
Church of St Mary, Clifton, Notts.
A.F.Kersting

119 **An unknown young man**
The Master of the View of Sainte Gudule
Oil on panel
The National Gallery, London

120 **Henry Stathum, his wives Anne Bothe, Elizabeth Seyntlow and his widow Margaret Stanhop**
Anon. English engraver
Brass rubbing
Church of St Matthew, Morley, Derbys.
Victoria and Albert Museum, Crown Copyright

121 **Sir Ralph Fitzherbert and his wife Elizabeth Marshall**
Anon. English sculptor
Alabaster effigies
Church of St Mary, Norbury and Roston, Derbys.
Canon Ridgway

122 **Female weepers from the Fitzherbert tomb**
Anon. English sculptor
Alabaster figurines
Church of St Mary, Norbury and Roston, Derbys.
RCHME

123 **Male weepers from the Fitzherbert tomb**
Anon. English sculptor
Alabaster figurines
Church of St Mary, Norbury and Roston, Derbys.
RCHME

124 **Sir Thomas Peyton and his two wives, both called Margaret**
Anon. English engraver
Brass rubbing
Church of St Andrew, Isleham, Cambs.
Victoria and Albert Museum, Crown Copyright

125 **Ralph Nevill, Earl of Westmorland, and his wife Elizabeth Percy**
Anon. English sculptor
Wooden effigies
Church of St Brandon, Brancepeth, County Durham
RCHME

126 **An unknown man, his wife and his mother**
The Master of the Legend of St Ursula
Oil on panel
Koninklijk Museum voor Schone Kunsten, Antwerp
ACL, Brussels

127 **Martin van Nieuwenhove**
Hans Memlinc
Oil on panel
Sint Janshospitaal, Bruges
ACL, Brussels

128 **The De Waele family (detail)**
Anon. Brussels painter
Oil on panel
Koninklijk Museum voor Schone Kunsten, Antwerp
ACL, Brussels

129 **John Barton and his wife**
Anon. English sculptor
Freestone(?) effigies
Church of St Giles, Holme, Notts.
RCHME

130 **A donor with St Clement**
Style of Simon Marmion
Oil on panel
The National Gallery, London

131 **A donatrix with St Elizabeth of Hungary**
Style of Simon Marmion
Oil on panel
Thyssen Collection, Lugano

132 **Willem van Overbeke with St William**
Anon. Flemish painter
Oil on panel
Staedelsches Kunstinstitut, Frankfurt
ACL, Brussels

133 **Johanna de Keysert, wife of Willem van Overbeke, with St John the Baptist**
Anon. Flemish painter
Oil on panel
Staedelsches Kunstinstitut, Frankfurt
ACL, Brussels

134 **A woman (detail from 'The Antwerp Archers' Feast')**
The Master of Frankfurt
Oil on panel
Koninklijk Museum voor Schone Kunsten, Antwerp
ACL, Brussels

135 **George Crane**
Anon. English sculptor
Alabaster effigy
Church of St Mary, Chilton, Suffolk
RCHME

136 **The Lover greets the God of Love**
Anon. Flemish illuminator
*Le Roman de la Rose*, Harley MS 4425, f. 24
The British Library, London

137 **A young couple praying before the Virgin and Child**
The Master of 1499
Oil on panel
Musée du Louvre, Paris
ACL, Brussels

138 **Pierre, duc de Bourbon, and St Peter**
The Master of Moulins
Oil on panel
Musée du Louvre, Paris
Musées Nationaux

139 **Anne de Beaujeu, duchesse de Bourbon, daughter of Louis XI of France**
The Master of Moulins
Oil on panel
Musée du Louvre, Paris
Musées Nationaux

140 **Suzanne de Bourbon, aged about two**
The Master of Moulins
Oil on panel
Musée du Louvre, Paris
Musées Nationaux

141 **Philip the Fair**
Netherlandish school
Oil on panel
The National Gallery, London

142 **Margaret of Austria**
Netherlandish school
Oil on panel
The National Gallery, London

143* **The King of France(?) with St Giles and the hind**
The Master of St Giles
Oil on panel
The National Gallery, London

144 **Jean, comte de la Tour d'Auvergne, with St John the Baptist**
The Master of the de la Tour d'Auvergne Triptych
Mixed technique(?) on panel
North Carolina Museum of Art, Raleigh, North Carolina

145 **Jeanne de Bourbon-Vendôme, comtesse de la Tour d'Auvergne, with St John the Evangelist**
The Master of the de la Tour d'Auvergne Triptych
Mixed technique(?) on panel
North Carolina Museum of Art, Raleigh, North Carolina

146 **An unknown couple**
The Master of the Embroidered Foliage
Oil on panel
Palais des Beaux-Arts, Lille
ACL, Brussels

147 **Hermann Rinck, mayer of Cologne, and his wife Gertrud von Ballem**
Master of the Aachen Altarpiece
Oil on panel
Walker Art Gallery, Liverpool

148 **An unknown Cologne woman**
Cologne school
Oil on panel
The National Gallery, London

149 **John Clerk and his wife Lucy**
Anon. English engraver
Brass
Church of St Bartholomew, Basildon, Berks.
RCHME

150 **Robert Serche and his wife Anne**
Anon. English engraver
Brass
Church of St Peter and St Paul, Northleach, Glos.
RCHME

# Introduction

This book must inevitably seek to achieve a degree of compromise between the objectives of its companion volumes, the study of fashionable dress mainly in England, and one of the realities of the late medieval world, the fact that England was not particularly important in the development of fashionable dress. In north-western Europe France, in the fourteenth century, and its north-eastern neighbour Flanders, in the fifteenth century, were the arbiters of late Gothic taste and magnificence. The splendour of the Burgundian ducal court at Bruges so impressed John Paston III when he accompanied the king's sister Margaret of York to Flanders to marry the duke of Burgundy in 1468 that he wrote home to his mother telling her that none of the men or women of the court was short of cloth of gold, silk, or gold or silver jewellery, and that he had never heard of any court like it, except that of King Arthur. In an attempt, therefore, to reflect the aims of the series and to reflect historical fact, this book will cross the English Channel more than once, and, in an attempt to show the diversity of northern European fashions, will even venture into Germany.

## THE SOURCES

The almost total lack of garments surviving from the Middle Ages relatively unrestored means that anyone studying the late medieval period has to rely on two sources only: the visual evidence, which records how people wished to be seen perhaps rather more accurately than surviving garments would allow us to guess at (which is in any case the essence of successful fashion illustration); and the literary evidence which encompasses the day-to-day business of recording the expenditure on dress of the wealthy and powerful; the outraged squawks of chroniclers and/or moralists when faced by new fashions; and the usually undated works of poets who tend to refer to dress in an unfuriatingly vague manner, assuming that the readers of their own day would 'get the general idea' of the dress they mentioned.

The surviving visual sources in continental Europe are almost entirely pictorial (i.e., paintings and illustrated books), while those in the British Isles are predominantly funerary (i.e., effigies, brasses and incised slabs). A painted portrait may well bear a date, and an illustrated book may well contain scenes of everyday life and people of different classes, allowing one to build up a series of 'coathangers', as it were, of dated or datable material on which to hang the stages of the development of a fashion, as well as an understanding of its appearance from different angles and its interpretation by different classes, according to the demands of practicality and purse.

Sculpture alone can reproduce the three-dimensional effect of clothing on a body, as its wearer imposes himself or herself visually (and physically, in the case of the enormous headdresses worn by women *c*. 1420) on those around, but the tombs and brasses have distinct problems as sources of information: they were sometimes commissioned within the lifetimes of those they were to commemorate, and sometimes long after. Consequently, any dates of death which they may bear, can be quite misleading if taken to represent the dates of commission. They cannot always be relied on to give an accurate likeness of the deceased, or any real indication of age, or even of social status: the famous contract for the effigies at Lowick, Northants, (fig. 59), drawn up in 1419 between Katherine, the widow of Ralph Greene, and the sculptors, stipulated that the male figure was to be a likeness, not of Ralph Greene, but of a fully armed esquire, and that the female was to be clad not as a widow, but in a '*surcote overte*' (open-sided gown), the ordinary dress for ceremonial purposes of a woman of rank. Thus if we have an effigy of a woman who is not dressed as a widow, but who is known to have outlived her husband, we cannot always be justified in assuming that the figures were carved before he died. One of the most curious features of the effigies is that they seem to depict people who are still alive, and who have been carved as though standing upright, before being laid flat on their backs, with the effect of gravity acting as it would on the dress of a standing, and not a supine, figure. When the bright paints in which the effigies were originally covered were undamaged, the sensation of the effigies being alive must have been profound. Because of the conventions of the sculptors, and because the effigies are being examined as sources of information on dress and not as pieces of sculpture, the effigies are mostly reproduced here as upright figures.

The merchant classes seem to have preferred as memorials brasses, or incised slabs, which were probably even cheaper, and they are so standardized in their representations (compare plates 84 and 104) that it looks as though either the pattern books for them could remain unchanged for up to twenty years, or they were more frequently ordered well in advance of being needed than effigies were – a practice perhaps made more common by the English custom of setting the figures and inscriptions separately into the tombstone. They too, therefore, have to be treated with caution as a source of information on dress, but these relatively modest forms of memorial may be a reflection of current social attitudes, not of real wealth, as a law of 1363 decreed that a merchant had to be worth £1000 before he could be considered the equal of a knight worth £500. The Lowick tomb, apparently a standardized product, cost only £40, well within the reach of a wealthy merchant, and Sir John Curzon (plate 107) left only seven marks to buy a brass for himself and his wife.

Finally, there is a tendency for monuments of all types to be concentrated in the wealthier south-east of England, although the brasses could be ordered from the London workshops and the alabaster effigies from the Derbyshire quarries for despatch to any part of the country. This concentration of the sources, both in place of production and in final resting place, makes it impossible to establish how regionalised dress really was within the British Isles as a whole.

In life, men had open to them a far wider range of occupations, and hence outfits, than women had, and yet the hierarchical nature of late medieval society, combined with the prevailing cult of chivalry, ensured that in death their options for the final image they would leave to posterity were far more limited. Most men of any social pretensions had no more indications of individual achievements, and even fewer indications of personal taste, to leave in their memorials than their wives had – unless they had risen to being barons of the Exchequer (plate 37) or judges (plate 62), in which case they might not be depicted as one of an endless series of armed men, but as members of a smaller group of men in official dress. At least women could, if they chose, be shown in the fashions and with the lapdogs they had loved in life (plate 37). Men had a chance to appear in fashionable dress usually only if they were in the subsidiary role of weepers (small figures of the family of the deceased, set along the front and sides of the tomb chest).

The documentary sources provide their own problems, the most obvious one being that of accessibility: they are often still largely unpublished (particularly the English royal wardrobe accounts), and the language used even in the published sources can be off-putting. The accounts were kept in rudimentary Latin or French, with the odd English word thrown in to confuse the modern reader, and the chroniclers, being mainly monastic, tended to write in Latin. These monkish sources, with their use of history to point moral lessons, are a joy in that they show the horrified reaction of the Church to new, and therefore evil, fashions, which God frequently chose to punish with natural disasters. One wonders, however, if only coincidences of new fashions and disasters were noted, and if other fashions and disasters were not considerate enough to happen almost simultaneously, they were ignored by these monks. Xenophobia provided another good excuse for decrying new fashions: John of Reading blamed the Hainaulters who accompanied Queen Philippa to England in 1327 for the ever-changing fashions of the next eighteen years (although the speed of fashion change seems to have been increasing everywhere at that time); and Anne of Bohemia, who arrived in 1381, was blamed by John Ross of Warwick for inducing Englishwomen to begin riding side-saddle instead of astride, and by the monk of Evesham for introducing shoes with long pointed toes, called 'cracows' or 'pykys'. Anne may well have introduced the side-saddle (the Ellesmere manuscript, an early text of the Canterbury Tales, shows the Wife of Bath sitting astride her horse), but 'crakowes' (sic) had been denounced in the *Eulogium Historiarum* as being among the follies of the year 1362. Thus it looks as though once again the chroniclers were not quite capable of distinguishing between coincidence, and cause and effect. Unfortunately foreigners took the blame for anything which their contemporaries did not like.

Even works in medieval English can be off-putting to read, because they look so strange, although they are less strange when read aloud. Individual poems, like individual works of art, may lack precise dates, despite offering delightful references to dress, such as the contrast between the kerchief, pearls and snowy-white throat and breast of the young lady, and the muffled head and neck of her wrinkled older companion in *Sir Gawain and the Green Knight*. This poem is generally dated to the end of the fourteenth century, but its only use to us here is its reiteration of a generally-held view of women in the Middle Ages – that older women were too ugly for anyone to want to look at much of them – and therefore it was better for everyone if they covered themselves up as completely as possible. Strangely, older men do not seem to have been regarded so unkindly. Chaucer's works have been plundered for references to dress, but the standard literary practice of his day, that of re-working or translating the works of other writers, makes this plundering a dangerous exercise. The pilgrims of *The Canterbury Tales* are presumably wearing the dress of Chaucer's day since they are his creations, but many of the stories they tell are derived from a number of sources, and when the narrator of the *Romaunt of the Rose* describes the process of getting dressed as involving sewing shut his sleeves, we have a reference not to the custom of Chaucer's day, but to that of the date of the poem's composition, over 150 years before.

## DRESS IN NORTH-WESTERN EUROPE

High fashion was frequently defined by law as being only for the upper classes, with a sliding scale of diminishing privileges from the royal families downwards, with occasional concessions being made to the merchant classes, who were, after all, largely responsible for the trade which created the wealth of their countries: in 1471 Scots women whose husbands were not quite wealthy enough to be allowed silks gowns, doublets or cloaks themselves, were allowed silk collars and sleeves, perhaps a wise acceptance of female vanity in a modified form. Fashionable garments, as they grew older and hence less fashionable, worked their way down the social scale, but not in the first flush of their modishness or luxury: in his will Richard II ordered the distribution of his robes among the servants of his chamber, but without their pearls and precious stones; in 1415 the Duke of York ordered that his 'hopolandres huykes' be given to his servants, but without their fur linings; and in 1483 Anthony, Earl Rivers, ordered that all his clothing and horse harness be sold to buy shirts for the poor.

Thus the garments of the upper classes might come into the hands of the wealthier middle classes, who, when they were finished with them, could sell them to the second-hand clothes dealers. That these people were not above 'fencing' stolen goods is shown by the mid fifteenth-century poem, 'London Lickpenny', whose narrator was amazed to see the hood which he had 'lost' in the jostling of the crowd at Westminster, on sale among 'mutch stolen gere' at Cornhill. Finally, garments would be worn out on the backs of the poor (plate 70). Even the mighty John of Gaunt had not been above buying robes from his cousin the Duchess of Norfolk, and in his will of 1397 he left them to his wife. Really elaborate garments, however, probably

14

never found their way, even altered, into fashionable use again: in 1439 the Countess of Warwick left her green cloth of gold gown with wide sleeves to Our Lady of Walsingham, and her wedding gown and most of the rest of her clothes of gold and silk to the abbey of Tewkesbury; and in 1449 Sir John Nevill, the heir of the Earl of Westmorland, left his gown and doublet of blue cloth of gold, his gown of black velvet and all his doublets of velvet to be made into vestments.

The Paston letters offer interesting evidence of how relatively short of clothing even the apparently well-off were in the fifteenth century, and how therefore clothing must be regarded as representing a greater capital investment than it does today. Around 1441 Margaret Paston complained that all she had for winter wear were her black and green gowns, the latter being so cumbersome that wearing it tired her. In 1448 she complained that it was impossible to get good cloth locally for herself or the children (even in Norfolk, *the* cloth-producing county in England!), and her mother-in-law Agnes sent instructions to London to check on the wardrobe of her son Clement: she knew he had five gowns, three short and two long, and if they were threadbare they were to be brushed to raise the pile again, a process to which the short blue gown had already been subjected after she had had it made from a long gown. His long gowns were already one and two years old. The shame which Margaret had felt for her beads when the Queen visited Norwich in 1453 or 1459 caused her to borrow her cousin's 'device' (a more elaborate necklace?), and provided her with an excuse to ask her husband John I for something better. In 1462 John III pointed out to his father John I that he had only one gown beyond his livery gown, and that without a change one gown would soon be worn out.

The posthumous inventory of the goods of Sir John Fastolfe (whose lands, incidentally, the Pastons were trying to acquire), drawn up in 1459, lists eight complete gowns, as well as bits of others, and may even include an old-fashioned houppelande, of cloth of gold ('a Goune of clothe of golde, with side slevis, sirples wise', i.e. with long sleeves like those of a priest's surplice), which suggests, as with the Countess of Warwick's wedding dress, that clothing could be retained if it were particularly valuable, regardless of its place in fashion.

The interest of men in their dress was apparently just as keen as that of women, as could be guessed from a survey of the gorgeous textiles worn by the aristocracy, but even among the middle classes the interest seems to have been quite intense. The Paston men worried about their clothes almost as much as the women: we have heard John III's worries in 1462, and in 1465 John I asked Margaret to find out where William Paston had bought his tippet of worsted so fine it was almost like silk, and to get him some for his collars, as he wanted his winter doublet to be entirely of worsted, in honour of Norfolk (Worsted being a place in Norfolk where cloth was woven). The famous French farce of Maistre Pathelin, written in the late 1460s, revolves around the attempts of the impoverished lawyer Pathelin to cheat a draper out of enough cloth to make new clothes for himself and his wife, and has Pathelin talking knowledgeably about the colour and 'hang' of cloth, as well as the quantity he will need. Since the cloth is the width of Brussels cloth (not explained), he will need three ells (about three yards) for himself, and two and a half for his wife, because she is tall. Such knowledge and interest in a man perhaps ought not to be so surprising, since to have new clothes one had to buy the cloth from a draper, and then take it to a tailor, both of which operations must have involved far more discussion than the buying of clothes need involve in today's chain stores.

The mobility of men of all ranks – as diplomats, merchants, sailors, or soldiers of fortune, helped by repeated English invasions of France from 1337 during the Hundred Years' War – meant that within the triangle of Britain, Flanders and France there was almost complete uniformity in men's fashions, but for women, however, the picture is completely different. Regionalization of fashion is very marked in women's dress, particularly, though inexplicably, in the headdress: when in the early fifteenth century the poet Alain Chartier wished to make clear the universal application of his remarks in his 'Miroir aux Dames', he addressed them to ladies and women, widowed, married and unmarried, wearing the hoods of Holland, France, Scotland and Germany. Dynastic marriages with foreign princesses or ladies of rank might have caused short-lived interest in the fashions of the ladies' homelands, but as a woman was expected, at least in England, to be absorbed entirely into her husband's family, so a queen was expected to forget her old loyalties and acquire the loyalties of her husband, the most obvious symbol of which was to dress like the women of her new country. In 1385 Isabella of Bavaria was made to change into French dress because her German clothes were too plain by French standards, before she was presented to Charles VI of France for his approval as a prospective bride. In 1389 Charles's brother Louis acquired an Italian wife in the shape of his cousin Valentina Visconti of Milan, but Valentina may have proved somewhat less tractable in matters of dress than Isabella, as shortly before her death in 1408 she was still adding to her wardrobe items, mainly shirts, from her homeland.

The expansionist ambitions of Edward III, however, offered the ladies of his court a chance to see some of the world, and his family are remarkable for their travels. The court was occasionally established across the Channel, and the queen gave birth to two of her sons in Antwerp (Lionel) and Ghent (John of Gaunt). In 1340 English ladies and the wives of London burgesses travelled to Ghent to see her, and in 1347, while heavily pregnant, she, with her ladies, who were anxious to see their menfolk and friends again, crossed to join the king after the fall of Calais. It is not surprising to find contemporary moralists remarking unfavourably on the masculine behaviour and dress of these 'liberated' ladies of the 1340s, and perhaps this peripatetic existence of her mother encouraged the spoilt and wayward princess Isabella to abandon repeatedly her Gascon husband, and return time and again to her father's court. Isabella's brothers sought their brides far afield: Lionel went to Milan in 1368 to marry

Violanta Visconti, and promptly died there, while John of Gaunt interfered personally in the affairs of Castile, to whose throne he had a claim through his second wife. John's son Henry, Earl of Derby (the future Henry IV), travelled to the Holy Land in the early 1390s, and on the way back stopped long enough in Milan in 1393 to become engaged to Lucia Visconti, who finally married Richard II's half-brother Edmund, Duke of Kent, in 1407. Henry IV's queen Joan of Navarre was also the dowager Duchess of Brittany; in 1404 the king's goldsmith Christopher Tilderley was paid £192 for collars (necklaces) set with pearls and sapphires that she sent to the children she had left there, and in 1408 she sent an English alabaster effigy to adorn the tomb of her late husband. This spirit of internationalism, a relic from the previous century, did not last long, however, and xenophobia re-asserted itself with complaints that Queen Joan was showing undue favour to Breton immigrants.

The English successes in France meant that for a brief spell under Henry V and Henry VI the two countries were one, but thereafter England seems to have turned in on herself, at least as far as the choosing of queens is concerned, and there is no indication that in the fifteenth century English ladies travelled as they had done under the influence of Queen Philippa in the previous century, or that the outlook was in general so international. The female figures on the tombs of Philippa and Edward III suggest a complete awareness of fashion trends in France and Flanders, even if the effigies of some of their female subjects show little or none of this awareness. The lack of comparable visual material for most of the fifteenth century makes it difficult to assess how aware English royal ladies were of European fashions, but the evidence for their subjects shows almost total ignorance of the finer points of foreign fashions in headwear. Elizabeth Berkeley, countess of Warwick, travelled extensively across her estates and to London between 1420 and 1421, but she made no effort to go to France to join her husband, who in that time ran up, perhaps by her efforts, an enormous bill of nearly £800 with tailors in London. The Paston women also travelled around their properties, but there is no sign that London was a normal place of call for them. Thus women's lives, and what they wore, were closely defined within the narrow worlds they inhabited.

## DEVELOPMENTS IN DRESS 1300–1500

Dress in the fourteenth and fifteenth centuries should almost certainly be seen firstly as a struggle to develop the mastery over cloth implied by the word 'tailoring', and then as an exuberant, ever-changing expression of delight in that mastery as the reality of the human form is denied again and again in some of the most fantastic fashions ever devised. The colours and the surface patterns of the textiles used also changed, and here the wardrobe accounts must be our surest guides. Brasses give almost no indication of these changes; effigies where traces of paint remain can be slightly more helpful; and illuminated manuscripts and paintings give us clear evidence of the shades of colour preferred. Throughout the period two of the self-generated rules of fashion apply with increasing clarity: the greater the inconvenience caused to the wearer by his or her dress, the higher is his or her status; and women, of whatever class, are always more hindered by their dress than are the men of their class, because of their less physically active lives.

Dress at the start of the fourteenth century calls for relatively little comment, as it is still based on the simple but potentially very dignified garments of the previous century whose attractions are perhaps best seen in the well-known statue of Countess Uta of about 1350, in Naumberg Cathedral, Germany. Those garments were similar for both sexes, being more or less shapeless body sections with tubular sleeves attached at the top of the side seams to form T-shapes, with cloaks on top. Women's clothes always covered their ankles, and sometimes trailed on the ground, but men's clothes could be shortened as far as the knee if violent activity were to be undertaken. Men's hair was also much easier to manage, being worn in soft waves with a small fringe and curls over the ears, whereas married women had to swathe their heads and necks in a series of veils. Unmarried girls were allowed to display their hair dressed in increasingly elaborate plaits.

By about 1320 attempts were being made to make the clothing of both sexes fit more tightly round the chest and arms. To help achieve this, buttons were introduced to the lower sleeves of the tunic, and the bunched upper sleeve was replaced by a three-quarter length sleeve on the supertunic. Where the shorter-sleeved supertunic was not worn, it is clear that the tunic sleeves were tight all the way up the arm; on top, women would wear a loosish sleeveless supertunic, open down the sides from shoulder- to hip-level, revealing the tightly-fitting tunic. Women's necklines also became more revealing as they widened.

Probably the most important development of the 1320s was that of a downward-pointing peak at the back of the three-quarter length sleeve; by about 1340 the sleeve had shortened to elbow-length while the peak continued to grow into pendent strips. Men's hoods also developed these strips at the back, and although the hairstyles of their wearers had not altered much, the headdresses of women had altered considerably, as even married women began to pay little more than lip-service to the idea that their heads should be covered: their elaborately plaited and stiffened hairstyles were too interesting to be concealed, at least at the front of the head.

Important changes began to take place in dress around 1340, with a move away from almost universal use of *mi-parti* as a means of making clothing more interesting, to an increasing use of embroidery, and the shortening of men's garments to just above knee-level. The increasing tightness of the garments of both sexes, as well as the shortness of men's, provoked reactions of disgust from older citizens, who saw only indecency in the change; what they failed to notice was that the dress of men and women was becoming less similar, although this point had been absorbed subconsciously by about 1360. As if to emphasize the parting of the ways, some men began to grow beards, which were accompanied by longer, more softly waved hair-styles. The growing tightness of men's bodices, achieved by the lavish use of buttons as centre-front fastenings from neck to hip, was counterbalanced by the flaring of the skirts of their tunics and supertunics, and by the introduction of dagged edges on hoods and hemlines. Women, however, had far less freedom, as dagged hems were incompatible with female modesty, and, although some of their skirts also flared from the hips, some of them appear to have been fairly tight all the way down. By now the pendent strips worn at the elbow were separate 'streamers' attached to bands bound round the upper arm, and, perhaps in imitation of the undulations of these streamers, by the early 1350s both sexes had developed a whiplash or sway-back stance.

In the late 1350s, perhaps from boredom, there began a move away from extreme tightness and shortness in men's dress, with the introduction of a garment known as the 'goun' or 'houppelande'; this was a full-length garment, buttoned down the front, and loose in the body although still tight in the sleeves. In turn, it was denounced as indecent, because men now looked like women from behind. Few of these garments, however, are to be seen, perhaps because they represented too much of an encumbrance after the years of freedom granted to male legs by short garments, and more important developments took place within the structure of already existing garments. In the early 1360s men took to wearing very short (i.e., hip-length) garments called paltoks, which probably were supertunics with the 'skirts' removed, and to which were tied *mi-parti* hose. The chest area was increasingly padded until it resembled an egg shape, and this new outline remained the basic understructure for men's dress until about 1410–20, during which time the goun/*houppelande* gradually asserted itself, until about 1390 no man of any social pretensions was without one. This garment is seen in varying lengths from the hip to floor, but is always distinguishable from the padded inner garment by the softness of its 'hang', and the width of its sleeves, which developed from simple tubes about 1380 to great open or closed funnel shapes, fashionable from the 1390s to about 1420. The sheer size of the *houppelande* made it ideal for developing various types of dagging on its hems and cuffs, and for fanciful treatment in general.

Until about 1380 women continued to wear tightly-fitting supertunics, with the front lacing of the bodice quite clearly visible in some cases; ceremonial dress required the partial covering of these dresses with an open-sided gown retained from the fashions of earlier years. By about 1360, in England at least, women had begun to cover their hair again; although there is evidence that the ladies of the English royal family preferred the rigid plaiting of the hair fashionable in France and Flanders, other English women, including the Countess of Warwick, were content to be depicted in headdresses which consisted of a number of veils with fluted edges framing the face from shoulder to shoulder, with or without a box-shaped understructure. By the later 1380s the veils were being draped only from ear to ear, or even from temple to temple, as the gown collar rose higher. This shrinking of women's veils under the influence of the collar was matched by a shortening of men's hair, or the curling of it at ear level, and, as if to compensate for this

loss of hair, most men grew small forked beards; as the collars grew ever higher, the beards had mostly disappeared by about 1410.

Neat headdressing does not, however, seem to have appealed for long to contemporary female taste, and by the mid-1390s small 'horns' of hair had begun to appear at women's temples; these horns developed to their logically illogical conclusion in England by about 1420, in headdresses so wide that their wearers appear to have borrowed the horns of Highland cattle to achieve the effect, and in France and Flanders, by about 1430, where they sat much higher and were more heart-shaped in outline.

The period dominated by the goun/*houppelande* marks a return to very similar outer garments for both sexes, although men's and women's gowns were distinguished by the lack of dagging on women's hems, and by the setting of the waistline about natural height for men and immediately below the bust for women. Women's gowns also developed very high standing collars about 1400, but these had to be turned flat on to the body by about 1415 under the competition for space from the headdress. Men's hoods, by now fantastically twisted, dagged and trimmed, were less of a threat to their collars, which, however, never grew as inconvenient as women's, although their hair was cropped very short as though the collars were a nuisance.

The frivolity of dress began to diminish after about 1420, when the dagging took on a more solid feeling with the outward turning of fur linings, and the gradual growth of padded rolls round men's hoods; as the rolls grew larger, so dagging slipped from fashion, and was almost entirely gone by about 1440. The skirts and sleeves of the goun/*houppelande* also shrank into the narrower lines of the slimmer, straight-sleeved gown of both sexes by about 1440; in the case of women's dress, it retained a V-shaped neckline into the 1480s, although by then the shrinking inwards of the gown could go no further. By the 1460s, in fact, it must have been almost impossible for a highly fashionable lady to breathe deeply or to move her arms. In men's dress, however, the impulse to impose tight control affected not so much the body as the clothing – any excess material left from the now shortened goun/*houppelande* was drawn into carefully set folds down the back and front, with a gradual fanning-out of these folds from waist to shoulder, and a matching exaggeration of the sleeve-head, so that by about 1450 men had become very wide-shouldered, narrow-waisted creatures walking around on long, slim legs which ended in the tapering toes of pointed shoes or boots.

In the mid-1450s the top-heaviness of the silhouette began to diminish, as the heavily padded hoods were slowly replaced by acorn-cup-shaped caps. Up to this point women had been toying with horned headdresses of varying heights, some very modest and others very elaborate, the size being a fairly good indicator of the rank of the wearer; but in the 1450s the urge to increase the size of the headdress seems to have become irresistible, as ladies sported tall horned or steeple-shaped caps, over which veils were draped or suspended from wires in shapes resembling huge butterflies. By the end of the 1460s only the tall steeple, simply draped, remained across the Channel, while the evidence available from England in the 1470s suggests that there the butterfly form, worn over a small pill-box hat, was the more popular design.

In the 1470s women's dress remained remarkably stable, with only the shrinking of the steeple to a small cap to mark the change into the next decade, but men's dress altered radically in this time. The bulkiness of the upper body had been discarded by the most fashionable by the mid-1470s, to be replaced by an exaggeratedly skimpy look where the sleeves were not joined to the body over the top of the armholes and the gown and the doublet were left unclosed. This slimness was increased by the reappearance of full-length gowns, and the growing to the shoulders of the hair, but, strangely enough, the tall caps of the previous decade were abandoned in favour of flat, brimless hats. In the 1480s men's gowns were simply cut more generously, until they developed true lapels on which exotic furs could be displayed. Women's gowns displayed a variety of attempts to move the waistline down from under the bust, where it had been since the start of the century, to natural waist level: in England, the eye is drawn unnecessarily farther down by the slinging of a loosely fitting belt round the hips, and across the Channel a narrow belt can be seen at natural waist level. A square neckline was introduced into women's dress in the mid-1480s, with the old V-shape still being represented by the neckline of an underjacket called a *brassière*, usually made in black.

Throughout the 1490s there seems to have been nothing left for men's dress to do, except to exaggerate its new bulky looseness, which it did to the point of what strikes us now as untidiness, with unfinished sleeve seams and gowns so loose and wide that they seem to be in danger of slipping off at any moment. The hair was cut in a long, square 'page boy' style, and at the other end of the body the feet were shod in square-toed shoes. Men had moved away entirely from Gothic spideriness, but not so women. They clung to tightly fitting, flat-chested bodices, even if they did now have square necklines, until about 1510; they adopted loose sleeves almost as slowly, with the cuff gradually loosening into a bell shape by the mid-1490s, and then the whole sleeve moving into an ever-lengthening funnel shape by about 1500. The small caps were covered in short lengths of black satin or velvet by aristocratic women on the Continent, and with linen veils by their less exalted compatriots. English women followed roughly the same idea with their headdress, but the undercap was more box-shaped and the veil was longer, requiring to be slit up the sides to allow its wearer to turn her head without running the risk of dislodging her headdress by catching it against her gown. With this reluctance to adopt a completely new design formula for dress, it looks as though the looped-up trains of the early 1490s were not so much an attempt to add bulk to the female figure, as a last defiant attempt to hold on to Gothic attentuation, but the battle to retain Gothic forms was probably lost as early as the 1480s when women accepted the square neckline. This demanded a revision of all the

formats which had gone before, and even the colours used had to change. The bright reds, greens and blues which had formed the basis of most wardrobes in the fourteenth and fifteenth centuries, despite the brief incursion of tan and plum colours in the third quarter of the fourteenth century, had to give way before more sombre colours, as black, which had always been a staple, though less prominent, colour, became *the* colour which all classes could wear and feel fashionable in; next in popularity was probably a sandy shade of brown, called tawny or *tanné*. People looked more solid in their new, squarer clothes, and colour had to be less frivolous to match.

The variety of material available for study alters considerably over the two centuries under discussion, and it is impossible to offer a year-by-year account at every stage; it has seemed to me to be better and more accurate to concentrate attention on the periods when most visual information is to be found, as this very wealth of material can be the most confusing by offering insights into the alternative styles of dress which were acceptable contemporaneously. This means that paintings and secular manuscripts become much more important in the fifteenth century, and so the fifteenth century occupies more space in this book than does the fourteenth.

Another problem, to which I have not been able to find a satisfactory solution, is what to call the garments worn. It would perhaps have been easier to give all the garments English names, but even the English did not always call them by their English names in the written sources, preferring French or Latin; and although the English used French words, it is still possible that there were minor national differences in the styles of the garments which now seem to share the same name, differences of which we cannot now be aware. The best solution seemed to me to be to call the major garments by their English names, where known, when discussing English dress, and to use French terms when discussing Franco-Flemish dress. To introduce German and Dutch terms for the few examples of dress from those regions seemed an unnecessary complication, therefore English or French terms are used as necessary.

The study of any period has its own peculiar problems, but the farther back one goes into the past, the more complex these problems tend to become, because of the almost certainly unrepresentative nature of the surviving sources, which are usually only aristocratic in origin, and because of our inability to feel much sympathy with people whose values are so different from our own, especially when, in the case of the Middle Ages, so much of the visual information on these people comes down to us in the guise of things the late twentieth century prefers not to think about, expressions of faith and acceptance of mortality. Even their aesthetic values find few echoes in ours, for, though we may be overwhelmed by the beauty of the great Gothic cathedrals, few of us would care to wear the dress of their builders, so alien is it to our images of ourselves. Perhaps the initial steps to appreciating late mediaeval dress should lie in wonder at the ingenuity of its designers, who cared little for practicality but much for splendour; the images on the following pages may help in this quest.

# PLATES & CAPTIONS

**1  A lady of the Heriz(?) family, c.1300–10**
Anon. English sculptor

**Note**  At this date it is impossible to draw hard-and-fast divisions between
the fashions of the thirteenth and fourteenth centuries. The structure of
the headdress recalls that of the earlier century, while its revealing of so
much hair looks forward into the later century.

**Head**  The headdress is the most elaborate part of a woman's outfit at this
time. Here it is composed of a series of (probably) linen bands with fluted
edges wound round the head and under the chin, while allowing the waved
and curled hair to show at the top and sides of the head. A shoulder-length
veil is worn on top.

**Body**  The outermost layer, which is not much in evidence at this time, is
a cloak worn out at the points of the shoulders and prevented from
slipping back and choking its wearer by the looping of the thumbs through
its cord at chest level; this is a relic of the behaviour of the previous
century, as is bunching up the cloak in folds and holding it against the
body with the forearms. Beneath is a sleeveless supertunic which fits well
around the chest and round the base of the neck, but falls loosely below
the bust. The arms are covered by the sleeves of a tunic worn as the final
visible layer of women's clothing; as yet, its sleeves fit only on the
forearms, and the bunching of the upper parts will be developed into a
shorter oversleeve by 1320. The combination of cloak, supertunic and
tunic forms the basis for the fourteenth century idea of a suit, known as a
'robe'. The underwear would consist of a linen smock and stockings, worn
with flat shoes.

**2  An unknown French lady, c.1315–20**
Anon. French sculptor

**Note**  The elegant gathering of the drapery to one side, and the placing of
the weight of the body on one foot are relics of French sculptural practice
of the previous century.

**Head**  The hair is drawn into two 'lumps' at eyebrow level and covered by
a shoulder-length veil, over which a narrow circlet has been set, perhaps to
keep it in place. A wimple is drawn up over the chin, to pass under the veil
at the 'lumps', and it also covers the space between the chin and the
neckline of the *surcote*.

**Body**  The cloak is still present, though less obvious; the drapery held in
the crook of the right arm is part of the *surcote* which is thereby raised to
reveal the skirt of the *cote* beneath. The *surcote* is still fairly loose, and its
sleeves have been cut off at three-quarter length to reveal the sleeves of the
*cote* which are tightly fastened by many tiny buttons along the forearm.
Buttons become a major feature of dress from now on.

**Accessories**  The lady wears shoes with slightly pointed toes.

### 3 Lady Joan Cobham, c.1320–5
Anon. English engraver

**Note** This figure shows an early attempt at making dress fit more tightly.

**Head** The hair appears as curls at the temples and is dressed somewhat unconvincingly into sharp points above the ears; these points have no effect on the angle of the outer edge of the wimple, which is presumably meant to be attached to them under the shoulder-length veil.

**Body** The supertunic is developing new features: a more clearly scooped neckline; three-quarter length sleeves with a slight peak at the cuffs; and a tendency to 'bind' across the chest as an attempt is made to make it fit more closely. As yet, however, only the sleeves of the tunic fit well, because they are so precisely buttoned.

**Accessories** Shoes with pointed toes appear from among the folds of the hem.

### 4 An unknown official of Sherwood Forest, c.1325–30
Anon. English sculptor

**Note** This figure combines fashionable dress with symbols of office, and it shows that the tunic and supertunic were basically the same for both sexes.

**Head** The man's hair, except for two sausage-shaped curls at the sides, is confined within a coif which has a narrow edging and is tied beneath his chin. This coif is probably part of his 'uniform'.

**Body** Around the shoulders is the hood with shoulder cape which remained in fashion until the end of the century. When the hood was worn pulled up on to the head, it looked like a loose Balaclava helmet with a small cape. Beneath is a rather loose supertunic with three-quarter length sleeves which now have a more pronounced bell-shape at the ends. The original supertunic would probably have been in *mi-parti*: when the future David II of Scotland married Joan of the Tower in 1328, his retinue were dressed in 'cloth of colour' (not described) and striped cloth, and in 1329 their household, even the laundress, were similarly dressed. When Joan's sister Eleanor married the Count of Guelders in 1332 her retinue were dressed in *mi-parti* of stripes and green cloth. Unseen but present beneath the forester's clothing would be a linen shirt, linen drawers, stockings of woollen cloth, and boots or shoes with pointed toes.

**Accessories** On a belt slung over the left shoulder is a hunting horn, another part of the 'uniform'.

**5 Lady Gobard(?), c.1325–30 (right)**
Anon. English sculptor

**Note** This effigy is usually dated c.1300 because it
retains thirteenth-century features in the canopy
overhead and the treatment of the cloak, but it is a
provincial work, and does contain early-
fourteenth-century features in the now
fragmentary kneeling figures beside the canopy
and in the dress.

**Head** The hair is allowed to show slightly as two
large lumps at ear level; they continue to serve as
anchorage for the crinkled wimple with fluted
lower edge. There are two veils on the head, one
shoulder-length, the other just on the top of the
head.

**Body** The cloak, which is drawn across the body,
manages to hide much of the rest of the outfit, but one
can still see that the supertunic is sleeveless and open
down its side seam to reveal a tiny area of the tunic skirt
and a minute square section of the belt worn between the
two layers at hip level. The tunic sleeves are tight all the
way up. This combination of tunic and open-sided
supertunic will become increasingly important.

23

## 6 Unknown Lady, c.1330–35
Anon. English sculptor

**Note** This effigy is usually dated *c.*1310, but the revealing of so much hair suggests a date nearer 1330.

**Head** The care bestowed on dressing the hair is now being shown off by drawing the veil back to reveal some of the top of the head, with the hair in a centre parting. It is dressed in two large 'swellings' over the ears and these are emphasized by vertical plaits in front. The veil is kept in place by a small circlet, and the wimple has moved down to reveal the chin. The whole head area has a much more open feeling to it.

**Body** The lady wears a sleeveless supertunic with a wide neckline and 'armholes' which extend to hip-level. It fits well across the upper chest whence it flares to her feet. Beneath is a tunic belted at natural waist height.

**Accessories** The lady has closely-fitting shoes with pointed toes.

## 7 A lady of the Vesci(?) family, c.1335–40
Anon. English sculptor

**Note** This figure shows the development of the alternative fashion for supertunics with sleeves.

**Head** The hair, which is just visible at the cheeks, is dressed in two curls at ear height. A shoulder-length veil with a slightly fluted edge is kept in place by a circlet decorated with flowers, and is attached at eye level to the wimple by a large-headed pin or stud.

**Body** The standard arrangement of tunic and supertunic is being modified slightly by the shortening of the sleeves of the supertunic to the elbows, where they have a narrow edging, probably of fur, and are beginning to develop a clearly hanging section at the back. This will lengthen into a streamer-like strip, known as a tippet.

## 8 Peasant women, c.1335–40
Anon. East Anglian illuminator

**Note** As long as tailoring remained fairly basic it was possible for the less well-off to have garments whose basic structure was the same as those of the well-to-do, but with less cloth and far less elaboration of surface detail.

**Head** The women wear hoods very like men's, with little points at the back. The open-fronted hood remains standard headwear for working class and lower middle class women in France and Flanders until the end of the following century. The woman on the right has a trace of a veil beneath her hood.

**Body** The women are working in their tunics, which are clear of the ground as working women's dress always was. The woman on the left has a striped sleeveless top of some kind and an apron.

**Accessories** The woman on the right has a purse hanging from a narrow belt.

**9  A boy caught stealing fruit, c.1335–40**
Anon. East Anglian illuminator

**Head**  Both the man and the boy have hoods, although the boy has turned his round and is using its point as a pocket for the fruit he is picking. His hair is fairly short and curly.

**Body**  The man wears a short, simple supertunic with rudimentary points to the sleeves. Underneath he has a paler, slightly longer tunic. The boy's supertunic has tight, full-length sleeves, and he has looped back the front of its skirt, either to make his climb easier or to serve as an extra pocket.

**Accessories**  Both figures have belts, the man's carrying a short dagger, and both wear dark stockings and shoes. The boy's shoes, abandoned at the foot of the tree, have laces over the instep. The man also has gloves.

**10  A girl having her hair dressed, c.1335–40**
Anon. East Anglian illuminator

**Note**  The thick comb used in the Middle Ages lies at the girl's knee.

**Head**  The girl's hair is parted in the centre before being plaited with ribbons and bunched up at the side of the head. The maid's lower status is shown by her having no such elaborate arrangement to disturb her veil.

**Body**  Both the girl and her maid are in their tunics, which still fit well only on the lower arms. The girl, however, has a lower and hence more fashionable neckline. The tunics are belted at natural waist level.

## 11 (?)Elizabeth Segrave, wife of Roger de Northwood, c.1335–40
Anon. French(?) engraver

**Note** This figure is usually identified as Joan de Badlesmere, wife of John de Northwood, Roger's grandfather, but Joan died in 1319 and Elizabeth in 1335. The hairstyle is more likely to have been worn by Elizabeth than by Joan.

**Head** The hair is waved to just below the ears and then plaited. The plaits are turned back on to the top of the head and are perhaps stiffened with wire to make them stand out at the bottom. The wimple continues to be tucked into the neckline, and to cover the chin, but the hair is freely displayed.

**Body** The tunic, which has decorated cuffs, can be seen on the forearms and above the ankles. On top is a very rare garment, which is like an extremely full version of a sleeveless surcoat embroidered at the hem and the 'armholes', and drawn up at the right. What looks like a patterned bodice is almost certainly an enlargement of a miniver-lined hood which could be drawn up over the head at the back and buttoned at the front; the buttons and buttonholes are visible on the inverted V shape at the peaks over the stomach.

**12 Female figure
from the Percy
Tomb, c.1340**
Anon. English sculptor

**Note** The plant life
above the figure's head
is a decorative means of
filling in the corner
space and is not part of
her headdress.

**Head** The hair is
dressed in deep waves
to eye level and is then
bound by ribbons into
lumps at ear level,
before being brought
round the outside of
the arrangement in a
halo effect which is
enhanced by the veil
with its semi-circular
front edge. The fluted
edge of the wimple has
been turned over to
emphasize the chin and
is draped quite tightly
round the neck before
disappearing into the
neckline of the
supertunic.

**Body** The lady has an
unremarkable robe,
made interesting only
by the star-shaped
buckle through which
are threaded the cords
of her cloak. These
cords are themselves
then elaborately
knotted at the sides.

**13 Male figure from the Percy Tomb, c.1340**
Anon. English sculptor

**Head** The hair is worn in a short fringe and corkscrew curls in front of the ears. The hood is worn on top and its point is now long enough to be brought forward and to reach almost to the wearer's left elbow.

**Body** The man is wearing a tunic which seems a bit too long and a bit too tight in the body for him as it crinkles and binds at the same time. The buttons and buttonholes on the lower sleeve are quite clearly carved. The skirt of the tunic must be open at the centre front, as was usual at this date, because it manages to reveal most of his right leg while concealing most of his left.

**Accessories** A purse with a dagger thrust through it is worn at the front in exactly the way Henry Knighton said dissolute women wore them when they appeared at tournaments in 1348, dressed in men's clothes. This figure also has short boots, laced across the top of the foot.

**14 An unknown man, c.1340–45**
Anon. English sculptor

**Note** From this time on the supertunics of men
and women develop along different lines, with
men's becoming shorter and buttoning across the
chest.

**Head** The hair is worn in heavy curls to chin
level.

**Body** The man wears a mid–calf length
supertunic with a slightly scooped neckline and
elbow-length sleeves with hip-length extensions.
It is buttoned tightly across the chest but flares
from hip level. The tightness of the supertunics of
the young of both sexes at the start of the 1340s
horrified their older contemporaries, who regarded
it as an entirely new fashion, not as a logical
outcome of moves which had been afoot for many
years. The extension of the use of buttons to make
the body of a garment fit seems inevitable, with
hindsight; perhaps it was their use in this way
which drew extra attention to the increasingly
tight chest area.

**Accessories** A plain belt is buckled at his left-
hand side and supports a purse at the centre front;
this belt probably serves to hide the seam joining
the bodice to the skirt. The feet are shod in ankle-
length boots with pointed toes.

## 15 William Lucy(?), c.1340–45
Anon. English sculptor

**Note** The dress of this figure represents a
compromise between the demands of fashion and
the demands of older-fashioned standards of
decency.

**Head** The hair is worn in a tiny fringe and curls
at the front. The face opening on the hood is
shrinking, so that, to get the hood over the head, it
has been necessary to slit it at the sides, and the
top section has been flapped back over the head.

**Body** The supertunic has the short, tailed sleeves
and close-fitting chest of fashion. The gathering
('frouncing') of the skirt is also in keeping with the
fashions of the early 1340s, but the length of it is
something of which the moralists would have
approved: young men were wearing them cut off
above the knees.

**Accessories** A narrow belt is slung round the
hips and belted at the front. A dagger hangs down
from this on two strings.

## 16 An unknown widow, c.1340–50
Anon. English sculptor

**Note** This figure is sometimes dated *c*.1310, but the cut of the clothes suggests a date not before *c*.1340.

**Head** The hair is completely covered, as befits a widow, by an under-veil and a shoulder-length over-veil with a slightly fluted edge. The chin and neck are completely covered by a closely-crimped wimple, tucked into the neckline of the supertunic. Such close crimping of a veil worn over the chin remained an essential part of widows' dress into the sixteenth century.

**Body** The lady wears the standard robe of three garments, with thirteenth-century ways of treating them, but the tight fit of the bodice and sleeves of the tunic, combined with the very wide-cut 'armholes' of the supertunic, places this outfit in the mid-fourteenth century. The supertunic is now recognizable as the open supertunic or *surcote ouverte* which survives in the ceremonial dress of the fifteenth century. It is sometimes called a 'side-less cote-hardie' by writers on effigies and brasses, but no such garment ever existed.

## 17 Blanche Mortimer, Lady Grandison, c.1347
Anon. English sculptor

**Note** Lady Grandison died in 1347; the effigy was presumably carved soon thereafter, as her husband, who outlived her, is buried in Hereford Cathedral. The way in which her skirt trails down the front of the tomb is said to be a local feature of Herefordshire effigies; perhaps the headdress is also a fairly local fashion.

**Head** The hair is worn in two vertical columns at the side of the face, under a fine veil which is kept in place by a circlet decorated with flowers. This veil sweeps down the cheeks, over the shoulders and then over the back of the arm, to finish near elbow height. Another veil is worn as a wimple. Over all this is a hood with large side flaps and peaked top, which forms a long tail (a tippet? or something more substantial?). John of Reading complained of the over-long tippets of hoods in 1344.

**Body** Here we see the new tight fashion for women, in which a dress with buttoned sleeves like those of the tunic comes to serve as the supertunic.

**18 Called Prince William of Hatfield, c.1344**
Anon. English sculptor

**Note** William, the second son of Edward III and Philippa of Hainault, died in 1344 at the age of eight. The dress of this figure, which offers us a rare glimpse of the elaborate textiles used, accords well with the traditional identification.

**Head** The hair is parted in the centre and waved almost to the shoulders. There is a small circlet on top.

**Body** The prince wears a cloak with leaf-shaped dagging, fastened with four large flower-shaped buttons on the right shoulder and flung back over the left shoulder. Dagging was one of the follies of 1344, according to John of Reading; he also disapproved of short, tight, buttoned garments such as the supertunic we see here. Although the surface of the stone is worn, it is still possible to make out the scrolling plant pattern of the textile; such a pattern could be woven or embroidered.

**Accessories** A belt with large studs and a large square buckle, decorated with a stylized flower, is worn at the top of the thighs. The legs must now be covered in tights rather than stockings. The ankle-length boots are elaborately punched with small cruciform holes.

According to John of Reading, women's dresses were so tight that their wearers had to use foxtails under their skirts to hide their rears; all we ever see, however, are skirts which flare from the hips. In any case, Lady Grandison has a cloak to hide under.

**Accessories** A rosary is held in the left hand, which has a ring on the wedding finger.

**19 An unidentified member of the Cockayne family(?), c.1345–50**
Anon. English sculptor

**Note** This shows a more conventional approach to fashion than the previous plate.

**Head** The hair, except for a roll-curl below the ears, is confined in a coif which is bound along its outer edges, and along what are presumably seams over the top of the head. The reason for wearing such a coif with ordinary dress is not clear. The man has grown a moustache and a short beard; according to Jean de Venette, men began to grow long beards in France in 1340. This was further proof of the degeneracy of the new fashions.

**Body** A full-length cloak, which bunches at the base of the neck, is fastened on the right shoulder and swept back to the left to reveal a supertunic which buttons down the front to the hem. The waist is drawn in and the supertunic is frounced from the hips to just above the knee.

**Accessories** A wide belt, decorated with large (metal?) squares is worn on the hips. It carries a tasselled triangular purse, and is knotted on itself after being buckled beside the purse. It was presumably still possible to wear stockings with supertunics of the length worn here.

**20 Guillaume de Machaut sings as his lady dances, c.1350–55**
Anon. French illuminator

**Head** The men's hair is swept back from the forehead, where there may be a curl or two, towards the shoulders; some also have long, unkept beards. The *chaperon*, if worn on the head, is turned back on itself over the forehead. The women wear their hair in two stiff plaits at the sides of the face, with two rolls at the back. The heroine has a small pillbox cap.

**Body** Some of the men wear their *chaperons* down on their shoulders; the women, however, have increasingly bare shoulders. Both male and female bodies exhibit a sway-back posture, and they are squeezed into very tight *surcotes*. Both sexes also share long *cornettes* which are attached to bands worn above the elbow; these are the final outcome of the extensions to the three-quarter length sleeves a generation before. The men also have long *cornettes* on their hoods; one man has had to knot his to get it out of the way. Tippets had been denounced by John of Reading in 1344. The women have small vertical slits in the front of their skirts to allow access to their purses beneath. Their skirts are never trimmed with dagging although the men's could be. In 1356 the Parliament of the Languedoc forbade the wearing of dagging, among other extravagances, until the king was ransomed from captivity in England.

**Accessories** The men have the usual belts and purses or weapons. Their shoes have openwork tops and are developing long pointed toes.

**21 Robert Braunche, merchant of King's Lynn, and his wives Letice and Margaret, c.1350–55**
Anon. Flemish engraver

**Note** This brass must have been imported during Braunche's lifetime, in the course of his trading with the Low Countries, as although Braunche died in 1364, the small figures in the feast scene below have the whiplash stance and short tunics of the early 1350s.

**Head** Braunche's hair is worn in large curls over his ears. His wives' hair and veiling can be compared with the basic structure of Lady Grandison's headdress c.1347.

**Body** Braunche wears his hood down over his shoulders, on top of a waisted ankle-length supertunic, slit up the front to the thighs. The tippets of the supertunic sleeves are almost lost against the background; they reach his knees. His wives wear much longer supertunics which they have gathered up to one side to reveal their lavishly patterned tunics. The pattern can be seen on the tunic sleeves to be a scrolling plant (compare plate 18). Their tippets stop well short of the knee.

**Accessories** The pointed tips of the women's toes can be seen; Braunche has longer toes on his short boots.

35

**22 Two unknown men, c.1355–60**
Anon. English sculptor

**Note** Both these effigies were originally on the one slab, and they must therefore be considered as offering evidence on alternative fashions.

**Head** Both men wear almost chokingly tight hoods, turned back round the face, and both have moustaches and beards.

**Body** The man on the left wears a fairly standard outfit of cloak, and tightly fitting supertunic with buttoned sleeves. The other man's garment is much more interesting as it is full-length, buttoned all the way down the front, and quite loose in the body (although it is still tight in the sleeves). This must be the 'goun' denounced as the horror of 1362, because it was long and made men look like women from the back. In fact, garments like this had been known to the French since the late 1350s at least.

**Accessories** The man on the left has the usual knotted hip belt with, in this case, a dagger.

## 23 Walter Helyon, franklin of Marcle, c.1355–60
Anon. English sculptor

**Note** Walter Helyon was alive in 1357 and this effigy probably dates from about that time. A franklin was not a particularly important person in rural society, and his clothing can therefore be expected to be a bit old-fashioned.

**Head** The hair reaches the shoulders and there is a pointed beard.

**Body** The hood is worn around the shoulders. Beneath is a supertunic so tight at the waist that it wrinkles there; the skirt section is more generously cut from the hips to the knees. This particular garment is interesting because of the relationship which it displays between the circumference of the area to be clothed, the tightness of the clothing, and the size and spacing of the buttons: the sleeves are the smallest area and have the smallest and most closely-set buttons; the 'bodice' and the skirt use buttons of the same size, but they are much more closely set when required to take the strain of the tight fit of the bodice.

## 24 Unknown man, c.1360–65
Anon. English engraver

**Note** This brass was re-used in 1570 for A. Dyson, which explains the lettering disfiguring its surface.

**Head** There is still a slightly unruly feeling about the hair which is worn in thick waves to the shoulders, and also the moustache and beard.

**Body** The cape of the hood reaches to the elbows and has two horizontal bands of decoration. The supertunic still has very long tippets, but in itself is shorter and more drawn in at the waist. The *Eulogium Historiarum* complained of silk garments called 'paltoks' to which men tied their *mi-parti* hose, the hose going by the name of 'harlottes' (worthless fellows), with the result that 'one harlot served another'. Three years later, in 1365, John of Reading said paltoks were so short as to display the ruder parts of the body. The supertunic of this man may be an echo of this disturbing fashion.

**Accessories** A knotted belt with a purse and a dagger thrust through the purse.

**25 A lady, said to be the wife of Sir John Jose of Clearwell, c.1360**
Anon. English sculptor

**Note** Sir John died in 1349, his wife in 1362; it is possible that she ordered their effigies towards the end of her life. They have suffered some scraping in the course of 'restoration', but their basic information remains sound.

**Head** The headdress is a complex arrangement of veils worn over a square-topped underprop of some kind. Next to the head is a veil with a tightly fluted edge, and on top are a number of more loosely fluted veils, stacked on top of each other. A plain veil forms the final layer. The whole structure stands clear of the head at the front.

**Body** The lady wears the three-piece robe which is now beginning to be reserved for 'official' dress as a statement of rank. It has a deeply cutaway supertunic, which reveals the shape of the body in its skin-tight tunic; this kind of deep scooping, initially introduced to allow women to retain a fashionable silhouette, is 'frozen' into the later forms of this garment, as is the vertical trimming down its front.

**Accessories** A belt is worn at hip level between the tunic and supertunic; this too becomes a 'frozen' fashion.

**26 Queen Philippa of Hainault, wife of Edward III, c.1365–7 Hennequin of Liège**

**Note** This effigy, for which the sculptor was paid £133 6s 8d in 1367, was made just before the queen died in 1367 in her mid-fifties. It makes no attempt to flatter her, or to disguise the fact that skin-tight bodices suited only the young and slender.

**Head** Although damaged, the headdress can be seen to have consisted of two 'columns' of plaited hair framing the face, with a band running between them. The whole structure was probably extremely rigid, and has more in common with the headdresses of contemporary France and Flanders than with the headdresses of her English subjects.

**Body** A cloak is worn out at the points of the shoulders, giving a clear view of the supertunic (or tunic?), with its wide neckline and centre front lacing.

**Accessories** A narrow belt is worn round the hips, and dips down under the stomach.

**27 Jean de Vaudetar presenting the *Bible Historiale* to Charles V of France, 1371**
John of Bruges

**Note** The king's outfit is like that of a judge and may therefore be disregarded in a discussion of fashion.

**Head** De Vaudetar's hair covers his ears and curls at the ends.

**Body** We see here the latest fashion in distorting the male body: a *surcote*, or perhaps a *pourpoint*, padded over the lower chest to make its wearer look like a pouter-pigeon, with a small waist and hips emphasized by the heavy belt worn round them. This garment has a small collar fastened by two small buttons; larger buttons fasten the 'skirt'; and the largest buttons of all fasten the 'bodice'. The sleeves extend over the hands and only in their upper part does the body have any freedom.

**Accessories** Tights with extremely long toes, probably with leather soles, and a long thin dagger hanging from the heavily studded belt.

## 28 Catherine, Countess of Warwick, c.1370–75

Anon. English sculptor

**Note** The effigy is perhaps connected with the rebuilding of the chapel where it lies; this work was ordered by the will of the Earl in 1369. The Countess died in 1367 or 1369.

**Head** The headdress is a fine, if highly stylized, example of the effect achieved by stacking up at least half-a-dozen layers of veiling with fluted edges.

**Body** The outfit of cloak and laced dress is very similar to that worn by Queen Philippa, but with less personally disastrous results. The lacing runs down the front of the bodice to the tops of the thighs, whence the skirt flares to the hem. The sleeves with their tiny buttons along the forearm reach halfway down the hand.

**Accessories** A narrow belt with studs shaped like small flowers is pushed down over the hips. The shoes have modestly pointed toes.

**29 Sir Godferey Foljambe, died 1376, and his
wife Avena, c.1375–80**
Anon. English sculptor

**Note** Although it is not the purpose of this book
to discuss armour, it is worth noting how encased
the heads of the couple look, despite the difference
in their headwear. Avena outlived her husband
and we have no way of knowing whether this
monument was set up before or after his death.

**Head** The inverted U-shaped headdress is
probably as thick a combination of fluted veils as
was possible, here stylized into a fretwork. They
are worn over a close-fitting undercap which itself
has a fluted edge.

**Body** Avena wears the robe of rank, with large
studs down the bodice of the open supertunic and
tiny buttons down the knuckle-length sleeves of
the tunic.

**30 A wedding, c.1380**
The *Parement* Master

**Note** This scene shows French fashions.

**Head** The men are clean-shaven and have their
hair curled round the backs of their necks. Two of
the women wear *chaperons* with front flaps pointed
at the chin; the pointed effect is repeated in the
stiff plaits worn in front of the ears of the other
women.

**Body** The men wear mid-thigh length *surcotes*
with tight waists and padded chests. The *chaperons*
are too small to be pulled on to the head; one is
worn folded and draped round the shoulders. The
women wear the tightly fitting dresses with wide
necklines which were called *cotes hardies*, and
white *cornettes* hanging from above the elbow. One
woman wears a cloak, which was a fairly common
thing for middle and working class women to do
when they went to church.

**Accessories** The men have belts at the hips, and
tights or stockings with leather soles.

**31 Joan de Cobham, wife of Sir John de la Pole, c.1380**
Anon. English engraver

**Note** Comparing this figure to the previous ones reveals that national differences in women's dress lie in the headdress rather than in the main garments.

**Head** The face is framed by a deep layer of fluted veils which are also fluted at the back. Headdresses of this type were probably constructed by using long narrow veils with fluting at both selvedges and folding them backwards and forwards on themselves at a length sufficient to frame the face.

**Body** The *cote hardie* is buttoned down the front and along the sleeves from the hands to above the elbows. It has tippets like those of its French counterparts.

**32 The two wives of Sir Reynald de Malyns, c.1385**
Anon. English engraver

**Head** Both headdresses are constructed from fluted veiling but with different results: that on the left is more usual, while that on the right is more like that of Lady Jose (plate 25), and also looks slightly more like the outline of Franco-Flemish plaits.

**Body** The overgarments, which look like smocks capable of being buttoned from neck to hem, are very unusual; they are perhaps the female version of the 'goun'. They are worn over tunics with knuckle-length sleeves; the tunic sleeves of the woman on the right are visible up to the elbow.

**33 Female weeper from the tomb of Edward III, 1377–86**
John Orchard(?)

**Note** Although the king died in 1377, his tomb was not completed until 1386. This figure again suggests that fashion for women at the English court may have been more French than English in origin.

**Head** The hair is dressed in two stiff plaits with a jewelled band, perhaps a link between their supports, crossing the top of the forehead.

**Body** The usual long-sleeved dress with tippets is made more interesting by the buttons down the bodice front and the pocket-like slits below.

**34 Male weeper from the tomb of Edward III, 1377–86**
John Orchard(?)

**Head** The hair is worn in a centre parting and drawn out in small curls above the ears.

**Body** The supertunic follows the usual pattern in its buttoning, but the chest is less aggressively padded than before. There appears to be no distinction made in the overlap-and-button arrangement in the dress of men and women. The rather tight-kneed look of this figure suggests the problems encountered by the 'heroes' of a satirical poem written in 1388: their hose were so tightly laced to their doublets, and their toes were so long that they could not kneel in church without great care for fear of 'hortyng of here hose' (hurting their hose).

46

**35 William Grevel, wool merchant, and his wife Marion, c.1386**
Anon. English engraver

**Note** Grevel died in 1401, his wife in 1386. The dress suggests the brass was ordered at the time of her death.

**Head** Grevel's hair is very closely cropped (or balding?), and he has the small forked beard which is coming into fashion. The frilled area of his wife's headdress is reduced to the stretch between the temples and the corresponding distance at the back of the neck.

**Body** Both wear undergarments with sleeves which reach the knuckles, and both have gowns which button to the hem and have straight sleeves. Grevel's, however, is shorter and is belted at the waist; his wife's has a high collar and flows freely from the shoulders. Grevel's side-fastening cloak may be a reference to some dignity or office he achieved.

**Accessories** The belt when worn over a gown is placed at natural waist level. The shoes are fastened by straps.

**36 Hantascia Disney, c.1380–90?**
Anon. English sculptor

**Note** This effigy shows that concessions could be made to make the wearing of fashionable dress less difficult for children.

**Head** The hair is enclosed in a netted cap, decorated with tiny roundels at the crossing points of the netting. Such a headdress would allow a child far greater freedom of movement than the headdress of women.

**Body** The main garment is an unremarkable gown.

**37 Sir John Cassy, Chief Baron of the Exchequer, and his wife Alice Giffard, c.1390–1400**
Anon. English engraver

**Note** Sir John died in 1400, but the dress is not quite in the height of fashion for 1400.

**Head** Sir John wears a judge's coif with his hair sprouting from it above his ears. His wife wears stacked veils.

**Body** The couple both wear closely gathered gowns with straight sleeves, the wife's sleeves being slightly wider and the collar of her gown being buttoned up the neck and edged with fur, like the sleeves. The undersleeves are loosening over the hands. Sir John completes his outfit with a hood pushed down over his shoulders, and a miniver-lined cloak. The coif, hood and cloak are 'uniform'.

**38 Richard II with St Edmund, Edward the Confessor and John the Baptist, c.1394–5?**
Anon. French(?) painter
See colour plate, between pp. 96 and 97.

**39 Angels wearing the livery badges of Richard II, c.1394–5?**
Anon. French(?) painter

**Head** Under their chaplets of roses the angels have longer and curlier hair than is strictly fashionable.

**Body** The angels wear baggy tunics with sleeves drawn in towards the wrists, such as were fashionable at the start of the century.

**Accessories** The angels wear collars of broomcods and badges in the form of a kneeling white hart with a crown round its neck, and a chain hanging from the crown. The collars may have a reference to the Plantagenet family (*planta genista* in Latin, meaning broom plant), but the original broomcod collar was that given to Richard II by Charles VI of France in 1393. Richard was widely criticized for his indiscriminate distribution of the white hart badge.

**40 The monk Philippe de Maizieres presenting a book to Richard II, 1395–6**
Anon. French illuminator

**Head** The hair is almost shoulder-length but the dandies of the court have fluffed theirs out around their ears, and wear jewelled circlets on top. Forked beards are becoming increasingly common.

**Body** The padded doublet of the mace-bearer on the left explains the shape of the chests of gowns of the courtiers on the right. Collars are beginning to choke their wearers and the cuffs of the tunic sleeves are widening into nuisances. The sleeves of the gowns are also widening. Dagging has been re-introduced up the side of the longest gown.

**Accessories** With the doublet the belt is worn at hip level; with the gown, at natural waist level. Hose can be in *mi-parti*: the parson in *The Canterbury Tales* denounced them, when made in white and red and worn with short gowns, as making men look as though they had hernias, and had had half their 'shameful privee membres . . . flayne'. The very long toes of these hose are rarely depicted but often denounced as having to be chained up to the knee before their wearer can walk; perhaps the chain worn by the man on the right is for that purpose. Richard II bought whale-bone for the points of his shoes 1393–4.

50

**41 Unknown civilian and wife, c.1395–1400**
Anon. English engraver

**Note** These figures show very clearly how the dress of men and women followed the same aesthetic principles at this time.

**Head** The man's hair, beard and moustache are all quite fashionable. The woman's headdress, a single veil with fluted front edge worn over two small horns of hair on the forehead, shows that some women had tired of the more elaborate arrangements of several veils.

**Body** Both wear gowns with collars buttoned up the neck and bag-shaped sleeves buttoned at the wrists. They also have mitten-like undersleeves. The differences lie in the vestigial buttoned hood on the man's shoulders, the length of his gown, its being open at the calves and its being belted.

**Accessories** The fashionably studded belt supports the short sword carried by civilians. The shoes are cut away at the top and have clearly defined soles.

**42 John de Oteswich and his wife Mary,
c.1395–1400**
Anon. English sculptor

**Head** The man's hair and beard are fashionable
and his wife has the new low veil with modest
peaks at the temples.

**Body** The man has a high-collared gown which is
carefully set in folds almost its entire length. The
gown is developing wide funnel-shaped sleeves
which hang to knee-level. Both wear lower
garments with sleeves which extend over the
hands. The wife wears the ceremonial robe of a
cloak, open-sided supertunic and tunic.

**Accessories** The man has the short sword of
civilians, decorated with the sacred monogram
'IHS' (the initial letters of the Greek for 'Jesus the
Son the Saviour').

**43 Edward Courtenay(?), c.1395–1400**
Anon. English sculptor

**Head** The hair is worn very short, as becomes
increasingly necessary as the gown collars grow
higher.

**Body** The doublet is still padded over the chest,
but the shape is less unnatural than a generation
before. It is fastened with large buttons in the
shape of flowers with four petals, probably
goldsmith's work. The hem is dagged in 'arrow
heads'.

**Accessories** The usual heavy belt worn with
doublets sits round the hips.

**44 Lady Arderne, c.1400**
Anon. English sculptor

**Note** There is some disagreement over the identity of the knight; is he Sir Thomas, who died in 1391, or is he Sir John, who died in 1408? The lady's headdress suggests a date, *c*.1400, which does not really help to solve the problem, and the Lancastrian livery collars perhaps indicate only a date after the deposition of Richard II in 1399. Traces of the original paint were recorded in 1852.

**Head** The lady's hair is dressed in an inverted U-shaped roll at the front of the head and encased in a caul decorated with (gilt) flowers and (green) leaves. The effect of small horns is achieved by snaking a band of flowers over the forehead.

**Body** The ceremonial robe had a blue cloak lined with red, a brown and gold supertunic with green lining, and a crimson tunic.

**Accessories** The usual belt at hip level and the Lancastrian collar of gilt SS on a green ground (see also plate 47).

**45 Chaucer reciting before an elegant audience, c.1400**
Anon. English illuminator
See colour plate between pp. 96 and 97.

**46 The Sun, by 1408**
Anon. English illuminator

**Note** The sun and the lion (Leo) on the chest are symbols relating to this figure alone, and should not be regarded as being typical of fashionable dress.

**Head** The length of the hair is dictated by the height of the collar; the beard consists of two tiny points on the chin.

**Body** The white gown, covered in daisies and violets, shows how short a gown could be while having trailing sleeves, which in this case are of the closed, bag-type. Despite the summery appearance of the figure, the gown is trimmed at neck and cuffs, and perhaps lined, with white fur.

**Accessories** The white tights have heavy pointed toes.

**47 John Gower, the poet, c.1408**
Anon. English sculptor

**Note** Gower's head rests not on the usual pillows but on copies of his works. The colouring is not original; at the end of the sixteenth century the gown was said to be 'purple damasked'; in 1719, scarlet; and in 1765, purple. Gower spent the last years of his life in the priory where he died and was buried in 1408; this may well explain his appearing slightly old-fashioned.

**Head** The hair is too long and the beard too pronounced for high fashion.

**Body** The gown is of the unbelted, straight-sleeved variety with prominent buttons, fashionable in the 1380s. This lack of interest in high fashion is in keeping with Gower's denunciation of the effect of fashion on the wearer, in his 'Mirour de l'Omme', written by the summer of 1381: vanity causes more concern about stains on clothing than about stains on the soul.

**Accessories** The poet wears a collar of SS, first given to him in 1393 by the future Henry IV when it was only Henry's private livery collar. The SS seem to stand for 'Soveigne vous de moy' ('remember me', or, 'forget me not'). Henry had a number of collars with combinations of those words, the letters SS and forget-me-not flowers. Gower's collar has a pendant in the shape of a swan, another of the devices of Henry.

**48 Unknown Lady, c.1405–10**
Anon. English sculptor

**Head** The hair within the caul is becoming much more noticeable at the sides of the head, and a padded circular roll, known as a *bourrelet* in France, is worn on top.

**Body** The collar of the gown is beginning to stand clear of the neck and to open slightly at the top. The 'waist-line' is situated just under the bust and the upper part of the torso is made to look fashionably small. The cuffs which flop back over the wrists may be the 'mittens' of the undersleeves, or they may be false cuffs attached to the smock sleeves. A cloak is worn to make this outfit more ceremonial.

**Accessories** Rings are worn on the outer fingers and there is a belt with a large square buckle. The shape of the shoes can be seen under the folds of the gown.

**49 Lady Elizabeth Blackett, wife of Sir William Wilcote, c.1410–15**
Anon. English sculptor

**Note** Although Lady Elizabeth was still alive in 1438, her dress suggests the effigies were carved about the date of Sir William's death, in 1411.

**Head** The hair is held in two cauls above the ears and a *bourrelet* with a meandering foliage pattern is set on top. It has a large brooch at the centre front.

**Body** A ceremonial cloak is worn over a closely pleated gown with wide sleeves and high collar. The collar is too deep to be worn closed, although it retains its buttons as decoration. The undersleeves are the slightly old-fashioned 'mittens'.

**Accessories** The usual high-set belt and the increasingly common collar of SS.

**50 One of the wives of Ralph Nevill, 1st Earl of Westmorland: Margaret Stafford or Joan Beaufort, c.1410**
Anon. English sculptor

**Note** The Earl is shown on his tomb with his wives in identical outfits. Margaret Stafford died in 1370, the Earl in 1425, and Joan Beaufort in 1440; the headdress, however, belongs to *c*.1410.

**Head** Under her coronet the Countess wears an elaborately decorated caul which forms two large 'bumps' over the ears.

**Body** The rest of the outfit is much more difficult to date, being the standard ceremonial robe. The outline of the supertunic's 'armholes' is emphasized by fur, which also forms the 'bodice'.

**Accessories** A narrow belt around the hips and a collar of SS.

**51 Lady Mainwaring, c.1410**
Anon. English sculptor

**Note** There is some confusion over the Christian name of the lady's husband, but general agreement that he died in 1410.

**Head** The structure of the caul is very similar to the Countess of Westmorland's, but it is topped by a circlet. A shoulder-length veil is pleated into a narrow strip and attached to the caul at the top of the head.

**Body** Lady Mainwaring wears the upper half of her collar unbuttoned and has undersleeves which stop at the wrist in a small cuff.

**Accessories** A collar of SS which look like twisted ribbons and a deep belt worn below the bust.

**53 John Urban and his wife Joan Reskymmer, c.1410**
Anon. English engraver

**Note** Joan is commemorated separately in another brass which gives the date of her death as 1414; this brass is to commemorate her husband's death in 1420. Nonetheless, the appearance of both figures suggests this brass cannot have been designed much after 1410.

**Head** John Urban's hairstyle is fashionably short and his wife's small 'bumps' of hair are draped with a short veil.

**Body** Despite the difference in length and the treatment of the collars, both gowns are basically similar in cut, with their flowing lines and bag-shaped sleeves.

**52 Clarice, wife of Robert de Frevile, c.1410**
Anon. English engraver

**Head** The fashionable small horns are achieved here by plaiting the hair.

**Body** The fur lining of the gown sleeves shows as a series of stripes, each stripe marking the division between the skins used. The undersleeves lack the falling cuffs of very high fashion.

**54 Lucy, wife of William, Baron Willoughby d'Eresby, and daughter of Roger, Lord Strange of Knokyn, c.1410**
Anon. English engraver

**Note** The Baron died in 1410, which is probably the date of this brass. It shows admirably the difference in the approaches to fashion of the middle classes in the previous plate and of the aristocracy.

**Head** The lady's hair is held in a fine net in two 'bumps' under a coronet.

**Body** The gown is a very lavish affair with its spiky collar and immense trailing sleeves, turned back at the wrist to reveal their lining. It is also far too long to walk in. In his 'Vision of Purgatory', written *c.*1409, William Staunton saw people whose clothes seemed to consist of nothing but dagging, or who had long 'pokes' on their sleeves, and women with gowns trailing behind them. The aristocratic inconvenience of this outfit is completed by inner cuffs hanging from the wrists.

**55 Brother Jean Hayton presents the *Livre des merveilles du monde* to John the Fearless, Duke of Burgundy, by 1413**
Anon. French illuminator

**Head** On top of their very short hair the men wear a variety of hoods and hats. They are all clean-shaven.

**Body** The Duke and his courtiers all wear *houppelandes* with high collars and wide sleeves; the Duke's sleeves are dagged and turned back to reveal the fur lining. Over his shoulders he wears a black *chaperon* decorated with small carpenter's planes, devices which also cover his *houppelande*. This badge he adopted in response to the threat implied in the badge of his rival the Duke of Orléans, a knotty stick. In 1416 Burgundy issued 80 livery *robes* covered in over 4,000 little planes.

**Accessories** The Duke has a chain with his devices round his shoulders, and round his waist a belt with a number of pendant chains.

**56 Louis II of Anjou, c.1415**
Anon. French painter

**Head** The finely dagged *chaperon* is being worn as a hat, with the *cornette* twisted on itself and wound round the head; the shoulder cape is gathered and pulled to the front. In England in 1411 or 1412 Thomas Occleve in his *De Regimine Principum* complained that more than a yard of broadcloth was going into the tippet of a man's hood, and that tailors and furriers would have to move out to the fields to find enough room to carry on their trades.

**Body** The seams of this red velvet cloth of gold *houppelande* can be seen quite clearly at the collar and shoulders.

**57 A lady with a
falcon and a lapdog,
c.1415**
Anon. Netherlandish
painter

**Head** Perhaps because
the lady is out of doors
she has a cap, with a
feathery surface,
instead of a flimsy veil.
The hair which would
normally be worn in
two neat horns on the
temples falls instead in
corkscrew curls.

**Body** This
*houppelande* is
interesting because of
its small collar and
sleeves slit their entire
length and then
dagged; though
dagging was used on
the sleeves and hems of
men's garments, it was
confined to the sleeves
on women's clothes for
the sake of female
modesty.

**Accessories** An
unusual necklace, like
'bubble' seaweed, and a
brooch in the form of a
flower. The lady also
wears a hawking glove.

62

## 58 Joan Risain, wife of John Peryent, c.1415
Anon. English engraver

**Note** Joan Risain and her husband were Bretons, naturalized English in 1412 and 1411 respectively. She was chief lady-in-waiting to Henry IV's queen, the former Duchess of Brittany, and her husband was esquire of the body and pennon-bearer to Richard II, and esquire to Henry IV and Henry V. The uncertain position of Bretons in England at this time, as well as a record of service to Richard II, may have made it advisable to make prominent display of loyalty to the king through the devices worn. Joan died in 1415.

**Head** This headdress is unique among brasses with its triangular structure and scrap of veil thrown on top. Women's headdresses do, however, increase in size very rapidly in the 1410s.

**Body** With the increasing size of the headdress it becomes impossible to wear the gown collar up; here it is spread over the shoulders, and the smock collar appears over it. The undersleeves are tight for a few inches above the wrist and then bell out.

**Accessories** A very high-set belt, a collar of SS and a swan badge on the collar.

## 59 Katherine, widow of Ralph Greene, 1419–20
Thomas Prentys and Robert Sutton of Chellaston

**Head** The hair, or something in imitation of it, is drawn out from the sides of the head in two very large netted horns, which are held together by a strip of net over the forehead. A veil is draped on top, and then over this is placed a *bourrelet* decorated with scrolling foliage and flowers. The bird in the centre of the brooch is perhaps a pelican, symbol of Christian self-sacrifice.

**Body** The outfit is that prescribed in the contract for the tomb: a '*surcote overte*', with the cloak and tight-fitting underdress which this word implies as complements to it.

**60 Beatrix, Countess of Arundel, c.1416–20**
Anon. English sculptor

**Note** The Earl died in his thirties in 1416 and it
may therefore have been left to the Countess, who
lived on until 1439, to order the tomb; the
headdress suggests she did this shortly after his
death.

**Head** This is the most elaborate of the English
horned headdresses, made more incredible by the
superimposition of the Countess's coronet which
was almost certainly never worn thus in life. The
hair must be supposed to be padded within these
great beaded cauls, whose horizontal thrust is
extended by some prop, perhaps whalebone,
hidden under the veil with the fluted edge.

**Body** The ceremonial robe is rendered
insignificant by the headdress.

**61 Millicent Bekeryng, wife of Sir William Meryng, c.1419**
Anon. English engraver

**Note** This brass was probably ordered at the time of Lady Millicent's death in 1419.

**Head** The cauls are the widest one ever sees. On top is a veil which appears to manage to have fluting all round.

**Body** The gown is still too long in the skirt and the sleeves for the comfort of the wearer, but now that the collar has been turned down, it is acquiring the proportions of a small cape, with the smock collar covering most of it. The bodice is laced shut at the centre front.

**Accessories** A small chain and pendant at the neck, and a narrow belt embroidered with trefoils and letters (sense unknown).

**62 Sir William Gascoigne, Lord Chief
Justice, and his wife Elizabeth Mowbray,
c.1419**
Anon. English sculptor

**Note** The effigies probably date from the time of
Sir William's death in 1419. His robes of office
were originally painted red.

**Head** Sir William wears a tight-fitting coif,
buttoned under the chin, with a tight hood round
his neck. His wife's cauls and veil are almost
identical to those in plate 59, but here the *bourrelet*
is extended sideways to echo the line of the cauls.

**Body** Lady Elizabeth's gown has the fashionable
turned-down collar. Sir William has thrown his
judge's cloak back over his left shoulder to reveal a
gown with fashionable pleating but with very
much narrower sleeves than are fashionable;
presumably the very wide sleeves would be
thought to detract from the dignity of his office.

**Accessories** Lady Elizabeth has a wide belt with
large square buckle. Sir William has knotted his
belt over itself at the buckle; it is studded with
stylized flowers.

**63 A lady receives a suitor, c.1415–20**
Anon. French illuminator

**Head** The man's hair is cropped very short. The
horned arrangement of the lady's veils is typically
French, and they would be held out on strips of
whalebone or dried plant stalks.

**Body** The man wears his dagged *chaperon* pushed
down on to his shoulders, over a *houppelande* with
dagged sleeves and hem; the dagging is continued
up the side seam of the 'skirt' where it has been
left open. The sleeves are covered in what are
probably embroidered teardrops, designed to
soften the heart of his lady. Her *houppelande* has
dagged sleeves and a turned-down collar which
sits more closely round the neck than its English
counterparts, although it too is partly covered with
the *chemise* collar.

**64 Two male weepers from the tomb of Lady Clinton, c.1422**
Anon. English sculptor

**Note** It has been suggested that the tomb is not that of Lady Clinton, but the date of her death (1422) and the dress of the weepers do suggest that the tomb could well be hers.

**Head** The hood is developing a small *bourrelet* round the head, although the cape and tippet are retained.

**Body** A greater stiffness is being introduced into the gowns with their smaller but rigid collars, the puffing of the sleeve heads on the left, and the smaller (and therefore less mobile) dags.

**Accessories** Belts, which are beginning a slow drift down the torso, a rosary and a prayer book.

**65 Duke John IV of Brabant, early 1420s**
Anon. Flemish draughtsman

**Head** The start of the *bourrelet* on the *chaperon* can be seen quite clearly; the dagging seems half-hearted.

**Body** The *houppelande* is as sumptuous as before but it seems less frivolous because of the way the dagging on the sleeves is now edged with the thick fur which also lines the garment.

**Accessories** A belt at natural waist level, and boots with long pointed toes.

66

le Duc jehan
Rrabant

**66  A fishing party at the court of Holland,
c.1425**
Anon. Dutch or Flemish draughtsman

**Head**  The hood, dagged in various ways, prevails
as outdoor headwear for men and women; when
women wear it, they set it over the small peaks of
hair at the temples which they also wear with veils.

**Body**  The dagging of the gowns of both sexes is
edged with fur, as it is on the *heuques* of the man
on the right and the kneeling man. The sleeves and
the skirts of the ladies are so long that once they
meet on the ground it is difficult to distinguish
them. Both sexes wear extremely inconvenient
dagged and trailing cuffs.

**67 Wenllan Walsche, wife of W. Moreton, c.1427**
Anon. English(?) engraver

**Note** The brass to this lady, who died in 1427, suggests that English dress was acceptable to certain ranks of Welsh society.

**Head** The side projections are shrinking at the base and expanding upwards to form a heart shape. A fluted veil is still retained, however.

**Body** The gown is laced shut between the edges of the collar. Although it retains most of the features of the previous decade, the gown and its sleeves are becoming less voluminous, and the closed bag sleeve is paving the way for much tighter, tubular sleeves.

## 69 Unknown Woman, c.1430
Robert Campin (attrib.)

**Head** The head of this young married woman is remarkably swathed considering her age: veils with tiny fluted edges are used to hide almost completely the small horns of hair; a veil is folded double and strapped under her chin; and another folded veil is pinned on top of the head. Towering horned headdresses had been attacked in this area by Brother Thomas Couette in 1428, and in Paris in 1429 by a Brother Richard. This headdress is perhaps a local response to the demands for modest headdresses, as well as a means to avoid giving over most of the surface of the painting to a towering headdress.

**Body** The rest of the outfit is unremarkable.

## 68 Unknown Man, c.1430
Robert Campin (attrib.)

**Note** This portrait and the next one show comfortably, rather than very, well-off members of the middle classes on the Franco-Flemish border.

**Head** The red *chaperon* has a small *bourrelet* almost hidden under the twisting and wrapping of the *cornette*; the shoulder-cape hangs over the left shoulder.

**Body** The outer garment is still finely pleated across the chest, and is tied shut at the small collar; the fur lining shows there and at the front opening. The *pourpoint* collar turns outwards at the front neck.

## 70 Catherine of Cleves distributing alms, c.1430
Northern Netherlandish illuminator

**Note** Cleves is an area close to Germany; the dress therefore reflects elements of German fashion.

**Head** Catherine's hair is drawn into two netted horns under a veil, as it would be in Flanders. Two of the beggars wear hoods which probably began their careers in the previous century.

**Body** Catherine's ermine-lined gown has the standing collar and cape-like hanging sleeves of German dress. To complement this volume, the undersleeves are full and gathered into small cuffs. The beggar child's doublet has the deeply cut armholes and curved sleeves of c.1400; it also has holes at the hem for lacing on the hose.

## 71 A lady playing a portable organ, c.1430
Northern Netherlandish draughtsman

**Head** Because she is out of doors, the lady wears a version of the male hood, smothered in leaf-shaped dagging, over her fashionably horned hair.

**Body** The gown swirls as lavishly as ever round the hem, but the bodice requires much less material than previously, and the sleeves are only slightly bag-shaped. The dagging hanging from the sleeves shows that this feature is no longer being regarded as integral to the garment.

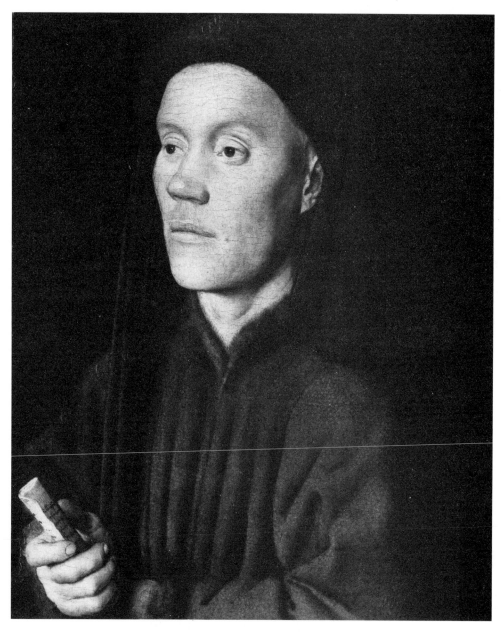

**72 'Leal Souvenir', 1432**
Jan van Eyck

**Head**  The dark green hood has a clearly defined *bourrelet*; the cape hangs over the left shoulder and the *cornette* over the right.

**Body**  The overgarment, which should now be called a *robe* rather than a *houppelande*, retains some of the front gathering of the latter garment, but without its positive feeling. It is of red ('scarlet'?) cloth, with a small fur-trimmed collar. Red and green were a popular combination.

**73 A Man in a Turban, 1433**
Jan van Eyck

**Head** The painting derives its title from the twisting and turning of the headcovering; it is not, however, a turban, but an ordinary *chaperon* treated in a rather extraordinary way. It is in the fashionable bright red.

**Body** The *robe* has a rather old-fashioned high collar, marking the increasing conservatism of increasing age. The *chemise* is just visible at the collar.

**74 The Marriage of Giovanni Arnolfini and Giovanna Cenami, 1434**
Jan van Eyck
See colour plate between pp. 96 and 97.

**75 William Welley, merchant, and his wife Alicia, mid-1430s(?)**
Anon. English engraver

**Note** Although the brass records Welley's death in 1450, the dress suggests it was ordered or designed about fifteen years earlier.

**Head** Welley's hair is cut extremely short. His wife's headdress is similar to that in plate 67, with an extra 'bump' in the middle, which is perhaps meant to indicate the top of the head.

**Body** Both gowns have shrinking bag-shaped sleeves; the collar on the woman's gown is considerably smaller than earlier collars.

77

**76 A weeper from the tomb of Gilbert Hay, Master of Errol, or of his father, Sir William Hay of Errol, Constable of Scotland, late 1430s**
Anon. Scottish(?) sculptor

**Note** Sir William died in 1437; his son predeceased him in 1436.

**Head** The dagging on the hood is so large that it looks like a series of flippers, and the tippet has been wound round the *bourrelet* to increase its bulk.

**Body** The gown neckline is worn open, revealing the doublet with its small standing collar and front lacing. The sleeves of the gown are considerably shrunken 'bags', and the simple dagging at the hem is fur-trimmed.

**Accessories** A belt now worn below the waistline, and ankle-length boots.

**77 A weeper (an armed retainer?) from the Hay tomb, late 1430s**
Anon. Scottish(?) sculptor

**Note** This figure is probably not meant to be fashionably dressed.

**Head** The hood is worn open under the chin, and the front is drawn back over something like a *bourrelet*. The shoulder section is dagged; in 1430 the Scottish Parliament tried to restrict the use of bag sleeves and dagging by the working classes to 'sentinel yeomen' riding with their masters.

**Body** The doublet, with its huge buttons down the front and smaller ones on the upper sleeve (purpose of those not clear), retains the hour-glass shape of *c*.1400. To it are tied stockings, worn over a pair of drawers.

**Accessories** Shoes with scooped fronts and buckled straps over the ankles.

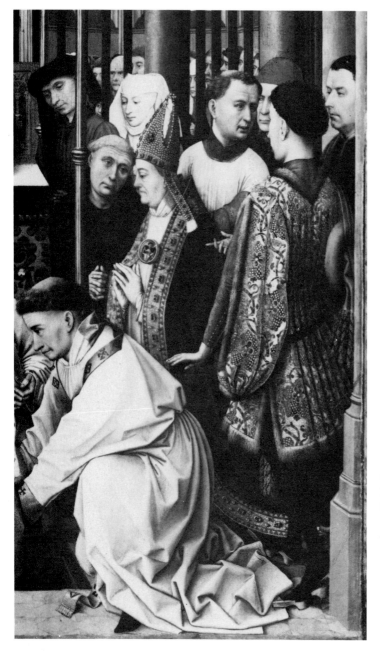

**78 The Exhumation of St Hubert (detail), c.1437**
Rogier van der Weyden (studio of)

**Note** This painting may show the headdresses of the women of the Brussels district.

**Head** The *chaperons* have pronounced *bourrelets*; the young dandy on the right has a very elaborately dagged cape and *cornette* on his *chaperon*, which he carries over his shoulder in the newly fashionable manner. Fashionable haircuts are still very short. Women wear linen caps starched into horns, with a veil on top and one under the chin.

**Body** The really fashionable man is gathering his robe into folds at the front and back, leaving the sides flat and slit up to the belt to give more material to the folds. The bag sleeve is slit vertically to allow the arm through before it reaches the cuff, and the back neckline is cut into a V-shape. Both these devices allow greater display of the *pourpoint*.

**Accessories** Stockings, soft ankle-length boots and pattens to protect the soles of the boots from wear on hard surfaces.

**79 St Mary Magdalene reading, late 1430s**
Rogier van der Weyden
See colour plate between pp. 96 and 97.

## 80 Agnes Campbell, wife of Sir Patrick Houston of that ilk, early 1440s
Anon. Scottish(?) sculptor

**Note** Sir Patrick died in 1456, but his wife's effigy is identical to that of the Lady of Lochawe at Kilmun, and that effigy is probably connected with the erection of Kilmun collegiate church in 1442.

**Head** This headdress is typical of Scottish effigies of the 1440s and 1450s. It consists of sharply pointed clips at the temples with a zigzag band across the brow. Over this is a fluted veil, kept in place by a *bourrelet* round which are entwined pearls(?) and flowers. The use of pearls was restricted by law in Scotland, to ensure an adequate supply for export.

**Body** The rest of the outfit is the standard ceremonial robe of north-western Europe.

## 81 St Mary Magdalene, from the 'Altarpiece of the Seven Sacraments', c.1445
Rogier van der Weyden

**Note** This figure is dressed in what was to become a 'uniform' for her and other young glamorous female saints, adapted from contemporary dress.

**Head** The 'turban' is the 'historicizing' part of the outfit.

**Body** We are offered a back view of the *cote* and its seams, with the waist, rather surprisingly, at natural height. The tightness of this garment shows that as well as being an underdress, it performed the function of the corset of more recent times. The *chemise* shows above the neckline and at the gap on the right sleeve between it and the paler, false sleeve. These false sleeves were usually pinned to the short sleeves of the *cote*, and were very often of a far more expensive material than the outer dress, to give the impression that the wearer was so wealthy that she could turn conventions of display on their head by wearing more expensive cloth in her underclothes than in her outer clothes.

**Accessories** A belt with a circular clasp, and a hook from which to hang a purse.

**82 Margaret of Anjou, Queen of Henry VI, receives a book from John Talbot, first Earl of Shrewsbury, c.1445**
Anon. English illuminator

**Note** Shrewsbury accompanied Margaret to England for her wedding in 1445. She and the King wear ceremonial dress.

**Head** The men still have very short hair. Their hoods have heavy *bourrelets*. The Queen's ladies wear horned headdresses with *bourrelets* on top.

**Body** There is a marked sense of order in the folds of the men's gowns, which are now knee-length; their sleeves have lost almost all of the bag shape. The Earl's gown is the most obvious exception to this rule, as it is his livery gown as a knight of the Order of the Garter, and its surface is duly covered with the badge of the Order. The doublet collars have squared-off front openings.

**Accessories** Ankle-length boots with short, pointed toes are the rule. Talbot and the man beside the King have collars of SS.

## 83 Edward Grimston, 1446
Petrus Christus

**Note** Grimston was an official of Henry VI's Household, employed as a negotiator with the Low Countries. This portrait was presumably painted on one of his visits to Flanders.

**Head** The *bourrelet* is now the most prominent part of the hood.

**Body** Three layers of clothing are visible. There is a green figured collarless gown, with vertical slits in the sleeves, through which the arms are passed. Next there is a red velvet doublet, with tight lower sleeves and puffed upper sleeves; this puffed section grows more pronounced in the next decade. The doublet is too skimpy to close across the chest, and is held as near shut as it can be by pairs of laces which emphasize the whiteness of the shirt beneath.

**Accessories** A collar of close-set gold links between the gown and the doublet, and a finer collar of SS held in the hand.

**84 John Lethenard, merchant, and his wife Joanna, late 1440s(?)**
Anon. English engraver

**Note** John Lethenard did not die until 1467, about twenty years after the date suggested by the dress.

**Head** The man's hair remains very short, and the woman's heart-shaped headdress is drawing its horns together.

**Body** Although the man's gown, with its bag-shaped sleeves, belongs basically in the 1430s, it still has the rising sleeve heads of the later 1440s. The woman's gown is easy to step into, with its long front opening which continues below the waist. Its sleeves are shrinking into tubes, which narrow at the fur-trimmed cuffs.

**85 An unknown young woman, c.1450**
Anon. Flemish draughtsman

**Note** This drawing shows the dress of a young married middle-class Flemish woman.

**Head** The horned cap is made of linen, and has a linen veil pinned and draped over it in such a way as to emphasize the horns.

**Body** The *robe* is at an awkward stage of being neither truly extravagant in its use of cloth, nor yet fitting neatly. The V-shaped neckline is trimmed with fur, as are the cuffs; a linen scarf is worn under the collar of the robe.

**86 Two female weepers from the tomb of Richard Beauchamp, Earl of Warwick, 1452–3** Cast by William Austen, from models perhaps by John Massingham

**Head** The headdresses have an outline of two small horns, either emphasized by a *bourrelet* with a small front flap and larger back flaps, or with a shoulder-length veil on top.

**Body** Under their cloaks the women have gowns with deep V-necklines. The neckline on the right is filled in with a stomacher, and that on the left by an under-collar or scarf, a low stomacher, and the top of the kirtle. The sleeves are fairly tight, especially at the wrists.

**Accessories** The figure on the left has a flower-studded belt, and holds a rosary; her companion, who holds a scroll, must be understood to be wearing a belt at a similar height.

**87 The Story of Patient Griselda, after 1451** The Master of Mansel

**Note** This and the following two plates, which come from the same manuscript, show subtle variations in the lengths of the men's hair, which can be explained not by their class, but by the artist's reacting to the changes in fashion during the years which it took to complete the illumination. This first miniature shows four episodes from Griselda's life and varying fortunes. On the top right while still at the house of her peasant father, she is asked by the Marquis of Salucces if she will be an obedient wife to him. Top left, she is married to the Marquis in clothes he has had made for her by referring his tailor to a girl of similar build. Bottom left, she is turned out by the Marquis in her underclothing, after he has decided to test her obedience by telling her that he has had their son and daughter killed. Bottom right, she is brought back to organize the household for the arrival of the Marquis's new wife and her brother, who are finally presented to her as the children she believed to have been killed.

**Head** Except at the wedding the Marquis wears a *chaperon* with a very thick *bourrelet*. Other men have shaggy flat hats, 'acorn-cup' caps, or a 'Robin Hood' bonnet. Griselda's father has a very old-fashioned *chaperon* with no *bourrelet*. Griselda as peasant girl and disgraced Marchioness wears a linen veil; as a bride she wears her hair loose, and as restored wife she wears a chequered flowerpot shaped cap under a small 'butterfly' headdress. At the wedding the ladies of the court wear larger versions of this headdress, while Griselda's daughter wears the uncovered flowerpot headdress of a young girl, with her hair drawn out through the top.

**Body** The men of the court all wear pleated and high-shouldered *robes* of varying lengths; Griselda's father's *robe* would have been fashionable twenty years before. Griselda shows the layers of women's dress: the calf-length *chemise*; the front-fastened tightly-fitting *cote* with added hem section (which could be replaced when worn out); and V-necked *robe* with tight bodice and sleeves, and very long train.

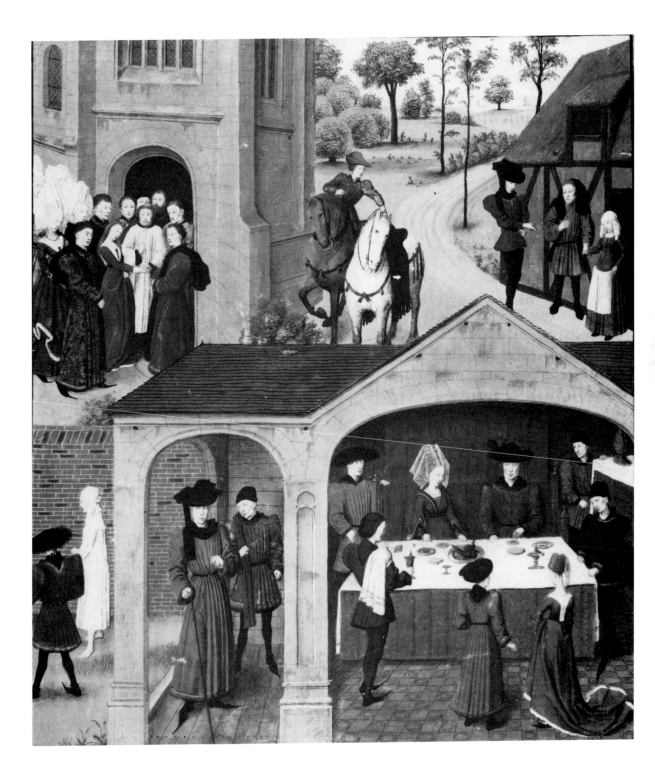

**88 People at Mass, after 1451**
The Master of Mansel

**Note** This scene contains people of different
social classes, particularly women.

**Head** The men have *chaperons* with *bourrelets*,
shaggy flat hats, or 'acorn cup' caps of varying
heights: the higher the cap, the more fashionable
the wearer. In some cases their hair is beginning to
cover their ears. The women wear tall horned
*bourrelets*, modestly horned linen veils, or the cloth
*chaperons* with *cornettes* which mark their wearers
as lower class.

**Body** The more fashionable men wear highly
controlled *robes*, with careful front and back
pleating and high sleeve heads; some wear short
cloaks on top. What can be seen of the women's
*robes* under their cloaks shows that the tightness of
the bodice varies with the class of the wearer and
that the well-to-do have V-shaped necklines back
and front. The *cote* has a detachable hem section.

**89 The marriage and coronation of Charles V of France and Jeanne de Bourbon, and the birth of the Dauphin, after 1451**
The Master of Mansel

**Note**  The events depicted here began in 1364, but are shown in the dress of the mid-1450s.

**Head**  The men's hair is now almost collar-length. The almoner of the Royal Household distributes alms to the poor who wear the *chaperons* of the 1420s and early 1430s and even earlier. The ladies wear tall steeple-shaped caps under veils held out on wires, like kites, or under a horned *bourrelet*.

**Body**  The men wear long *robes* because of the dignity of the events in the foreground; in the background, again the dress of the poor is hopelessly out of date. The ladies are in tight-bodiced and tight-sleeved *robes* with long trains kilted up for walking, over ground-length *cotes*; or *surcotes ouvertes* with white fur-trimmed bodices and darker skirts, over tight *cotes*.

**Accessories**  Belts for both sexes, chains and necklaces for the ladies, and shoes with long pointed toes; the men wear longer toes because their dress is not as consistently round their feet as women's is.

**90 The granting of privileges to Ghent and Flanders, after 1453**
Anon. Flemish illuminator

**Note** The man to the left of the throne is in legal dress, based on the dress of the previous century.

**Head** The variety of headwear for men is typical of the 1450s. The ladies have very tall, patterned, horned headdresses with veils on top like butterflies, or with *bourrelets*, dagged 'capes' at the back, and *cornettes* which can be strapped round the chin.

**Body** The *robes* of the kneeling citizens lack the highly fashionable exaggerations of wide shoulders and narrow waists of the Count and his courtiers. The necklines of the ladies' *robes* are moving out to the points of their shoulders at the front, but are firmly anchored at the back, where an extra piece of fur hangs free in a V-shape to continue the effect of the front-neckline. Even the long trains of their *robes* terminate in V-shapes.

**Accessories** The men wear narrow belts with daggers; the ladies wear deeper belts round impossibly narrow ribcages, with strings of beads to fill in the bare neckline.

**91 Lady Elizabeth Keith, daughter of the Marischal of Scotland and wife of Sir Alexander Irvine of Drum, c.1455**
Anon. Scottish(?) sculptor

**Note** The effigies of the couple are probably connected with Sir Alexander's grant in 1455 to the altar in front of which they lay; Sir Alexander died in 1457.

**Head** This headdress retains the zigzag browband and the fretted cheek-clips of the Lady of Houston (plate 80), although the clips here are less spiky. The beaded roll which keeps the veil in place is drawn into small horns.

**Body** The gown, with its wide flat collar, carefully set folds and wide sleeves, is still of the *houppelande* type; perhaps this was what so startled the Burgundian visitors who came to Scotland in 1449 to attend the wedding of James II and Mary of Guelders.

**Accessories** A double row of beads (pearls?) supports a pendant, and several rings are worn.

**92 Unknown young woman, c.1450–55**
Petrus Christus (attrib.)

**Head** This setting of the veil over two splayed horns is quite common in well-to-do Flemish dress.

**Body** The gown is still loose in the sleeves, but impossibly narrow in the body. It is laced shut over a scarf which covers the upper chest, and has a wide fur collar.

**94 Flemish street scene, with presentation of a book to Philip the Good of Burgundy in the background, c.1460**
Jean le Tavernier

**Note** The curious posture of the men is Tavernier's own reaction to the effect of padding in the sleeveheads.

**Head** Fashionable men have abandoned the *chaperon* for hats, although some keep the *cornette* attached to these hats. Tradesmen still wear very old-fashioned *chaperons*. The working women wear *chaperons* with front flaps.

**Body** The pleating and padding of men's dress has given them an extremely unnatural shape, whose apparent discomfort must be increased by the too-long sleeves. The scooping out of the back neckline appears to be genuine in some cases, allowing the *pourpoint* collar to show, but in others is no more than a vestige of the practice, with the standing collar being part of the *robe*. Short capes can be worn on top of short *robes*.

**Accessories** The hose are carefully seamed down the back of the legs, and on the feet are ankle-length boots, sometimes protected by pattens. No elegant man can afford to be without a walking stick to lean on, although a sword may provide an acceptable substitute.

**93 Richard Manfeld, his sister Isabel and his brother John (in a shroud), 1455**
Anon. English engraver

**Head** Richard's hair is still very short; his sister wears her hair loose in token of her virginity.

**Body** Richard's knee-length gown with its slightly gathered and raised sleeve heads and moderately drawn-in waist is a modified version of high fashion. His sister wears the ceremonial robe.

**95  Philip the Good, Duke of Burgundy, and the Duchess, Isabella of Portugal, at prayer with their courtiers, c.1460**
Anon. Flemish illuminator

**Head**  The men's hair is beginning to grow down over their ears. The women wear small caps with veils drawn straight round or into two small 'wings', or with a *bourrelet*.

**Body**  The men's robes follow the standard pattern of pleating and wide shoulders. The women's necklines have reached the points of their shoulders, and must need the tightness of the sleeves to stay in place. The cuffs are becoming increasingly important.

**Accessories**  The Duke carries his hat on a *cornette* and wears the collar of the Order of the Golden Fleece. The ladies wear wide collar-like necklaces under flimsy scarves, partly to hide and partly to emphasize their bare necks and shoulders.

**96  Portrait of an unknown young woman, c.1460**
Rogier van der Weyden (studio of)
See colour plate between pp. 96 and 97.

**97 Joan, wife of William Canyng, merchant and mayor of Bristol, c.1460**
Anon. English sculptor

**Note** Joan Canyng died in 1460; the attire, which is not nearly as revealing or tight as that of the ladies of the Burgundian court, is compatible with that of prosperous middle-class women of about that date.

**Head** The headdress is a simple arrangement of veils, worn over a slightly box-shaped understructure set on top of the head.

**Body** The gown has the usual V-neck, trimmed with fur, and has unfashionably long and baggy sleeves. Underneath is a kirtle with a remarkably high neckline, laced down the centre front. What looks like a square neckline continuing round the neck, is almost certainly the edge of a scarf, which would have been clearly defined by the paint on the effigy.

**Accessories** The belt is too narrow and too long for high fashion.

**98 William Canynge, husband of Joan Canynge, c.1460**
Anon. English sculptor

**Note** In 1467 William Canynge became a priest and then dean of the College of Westbury; there is a second, later effigy of him in his clerical robes. This effigy presumably shows him in his robes as mayor of Bristol, or in the livery of the merchants' guild.

**Head** He is too bald to be able to pay any attention to fashionable hairdressing.

**Body** The layers of dress are rather difficult to disentangle, but he appears to be wearing a doublet with a high collar under an ankle-length gown with loosish sleeves, trimmed at wrists and hem with narrow fur borders. On top is a semi-circular cloak, fastened on his right shoulders, also trimmed with a narrow fur border which disappears when the cloak is folded back on itself about knee-height, before being gathered up on the left shoulder. Its relationship to the outer collar is not clear, but it looks as though the collar helps to keep it in place there.

**Accessories** He carries a hood with a small *bourrelet* and long tippet over his left shoulder; such hoods continued to be used in liveries and cermonial dress long after they had ceased to be fashionable.

**99 Heinrich Blarer, 1460**
Anon. South German painter

**Note** This young man is wearing south German dress.

**Head** A large hat made of two different colours of fur, sits on top of the long wavy hair which is characteristic of south German fashion.

**Body** The main garment is rather ill-defined, but may be related to the robes of the Order of the Jar, founded in honour of the Virgin Mary, whose members had to wear their robes on Saturdays, the day of the week dedicated to the Virgin; the sash is that of the Order. Beneath is a doublet with a collar which comes very far forward and stands very high by Franco-Flemish (and English) standards; it is laced shut through a series of rings.

**38   Richard II with Sts Edmund, Edward the Confessor and John the Baptist, 1394-5(?)**
Anon. French(?) painter

**Note** The date of this painting has been the subject of much debate, but the dress suggests a date in the 1390s.

**Head** The hair and beards, except for those of the ascetic Baptist, are worn in variations on the prevailing style.

**Body** St Edmund and St Edward have cloaks lined and trimmed with ermine, as befits their regal status. They both have mitten-like cuffs on their tunic sleeves, those of St Edmund being so loose that they flap back on themselves. This saint and Richard II wear gowns with very wide, hanging sleeves; although the textiles of both show the fashion for patterns enclosed in circular outlines, Richard's is very personal with its harts encircled by broomcods (see plate 39). Richard's sleeves are lined with white fur; unusually, fringing is used on the collar instead of fur, and this fringing is repeated round the armhole and down the sleeve seam. Richard was notorious for his love of fine clothes, and was often accused of leading his subjects into extravagant habits. He is said to have had a tunic worth 30,000 marks, covered in gold and precious stones.

**Accessories** The three kings wear crowns and Richard wears his livery collar and badge (see plate 39).

**45 Chaucer reciting before an elegant audience, c.1400**
Anon. English illuminator

**Note** The sheer impracticality of the dress worn here suggests that here we see the royal court, where looking splendid was far more important that being able to do anything for oneself.

**Head** The men who are not bare-headed wear hoods flat on top of their heads as if they were hats, with the capes and tippets twisted into fantastic shapes. The women wear their hair scraped up into little lumps above the ears and decorated in front with curved gold bands.

**Body** Both men and women wear gowns with high collars and trailing sleeves; the woman on the bottom left cannot get her hands out of hers. Sleeves like this provoked much adverse criticism, especially when worn by servants who, after sweeping the streets with them, would proceed to drop them into the food they were serving, and in 1402 Parliament petitioned the king to prohibit their use, along with gowns which reached the ground, to anyone below the rank of knight banneret.

**Accessories** There is a profusion of gold belts and chains, with and without small bells.

## 74 The Marriage of Giovanni Arnolfini and Giovanna Cenami, 1434
Jan van Eyck

**Note** The couple were Italians living, before their marriage, in Bruges and Paris respectively, because of their connections with the Italian silk trade. The bride is wearing Flemish, not Italian, dress; her headdress may even be peculiar to Bruges.

**Head** The bridegroom's large hat is fairly unusual; this one is made of straw. The bride's hair is worn in two netted horns, under five layers of fluted veiling.

**Body** The man wears a plum-coloured *heuque*, cut from sections of a circle. This is lined and trimmed with brown fur. Underneath he has a black doublet with a standing collar and loose sleeves, gathered into narrow cuffs. The woman's dress is unusually ostentatious in its length (she has to bunch it up in front of her to walk), in its long train, and in its great bag sleeves, trimmed with many strips of dagged cloth. Its green colour was probably chosen to symbolize the freshness of her love, while the blue of the *cote* would symbolize the loyalty of that love.

**79   St Mary Magdalene reading, late 1430s**
Rogier van der Weyden

**Head** The fluted veil, with its turban-like draping, is van der Weyden's standard adaptation of contemporary headwear for a non-contemporary figure.

**Body** The olive green *robe*, drawn up at the knees to reveal its grey fur lining and the cloth-of-gold *cote*, still has carefully set folds above and below the high waistline. The neckline is a narrow V, trimmed with grey fur and laced across, over the top of the *cote*. Beneath the *cote* is a linen scarf, to protect the fur from the body. Despite all this orderliness, the sleeves are very long and loose, and still slightly bag-shaped.

**Accessories** A long, dark blue damask-woven silk belt trails its intricately worked metal end on the floor.

## 96　An unknown young woman, c.1460
Rogier van der Weyden (studio of)

**Note** This sitter is fairly well-off and fashionable, but the subdued colouring of her *robe* suggests that she is not aristocratic.

**Head** The cap is a cross between the horned headdress and the steeple headdress. The unnaturally high forehead is emphasized by the continuation of the veil down to the eyebrows.

**Body** The *robe* is trimmed at collar and cuffs with patterned velvet or damask, and demands stick-like arms. The expanse of chest which it would leave bare is covered by a velvet *pièce*, and the rest of the neckline is filled in by a scarf of similar thickness to the veil; it is pinned together at the base of the throat by a pin of about the same size as that used to create the 'horns' on the headdress. Beneath is a black cord whose function is not clear.

**Accessories** Although there are two rings placed on the second knuckle of the 'wedding finger', suggesting a fine disregard for manual labour, the quality of the rings is fairly modest, in keeping with the limited use of silk fabrics in the rest of the outfit.

**114 Sir John Donne, c.1477**
Hans Memlinc

**Note** Sir John was presumably painted by Memlinc on a diplomatic visit to Flanders for Edward IV.

**Head** Sir John tries, with his thinning hair, to wear the fashionable longer, shaggy hairstyle, which only young men could be sure of achieving.

**Body** The outfit is responding to the call for skimpily cut garments: here the velvet gown has vertical slits in the upper arms to allow for movement, and because the gown is not closed, its front edges roll back on themselves to form the start of lapels as a fashionable feature. The skin-tight doublet reveals the front of the shirt behind its black laces.

**Accessories** Sir John wears one ring and the Yorkist livery collar of suns and roses with a heraldic lion pendant.

**115 Lady Donne and her daughter, c.1477**
Hans Memlinc

**Note** It is unlikely that Lady Donne ever wore Flemish dress, which we see here, but her outfit is a good example of contemporary Flemish fashions, and her daughter's dress shows that children were not always dressed in smaller versions of their parents' clothes.

**Head** Lady Donne and her daughter both wear a velvet frontlet with a small loop at the front. The child is allowed the greater freedom of wearing her hair pulled through the frontlet, with no further inconveniences, but her mother's hair must be contained in the tall cone which is inserted into the back of the frontlet. On top is a transparent floor-length veil.

**Body** Lady Donne wears a fashionable gown, with ermine collar and hem. The front lacing on her daughter's gown can be loosened as she grows, and she is not squeezed into a tight, deep belt like her mother's.

**Accessories** Lady Donne also wears the Yorkist collar, with a tiny black cord at the base of her neck; her daughter has a brooch pinned to her frontlet.

**143 The King of France(?) with St Giles and the hind**
**c.1495–1500**
The Master of St Giles

**Note** This painting shows the way in which men wrapped somewhat-too-big garments around their bodies to make themselves look more solid.

**Head** Velvet bonnets with turned-up back sections, or hats with halo brims sit on top of long, fluffy hair, sometimes at an angle.

**Body** The robe of the King(?) is of bottle green velvet, lined with red velvet cloth-of-gold; the sleeve and armhole seams are left partly unsewn so that the lining falls back in a shape which echoes that of the lapels. Some of the attendants wear *cotes*(?) with fitted bodices and pleated skirts.

**Accessories** The shoes and thigh-length boots are made of soft leather and have rounded toes.

## 100 An unknown man, 1462
Dirk Bouts

**Head** The acorn-cup cap, probably made of felt, is growing taller, and has a small 'stalk' on its summit. The hair is worn to the collar, and fluffed out over the ears.

**Body** Once again, the main garment is rather mysterious: it seems to be a cloak slung to one side, covering all but the cuff of the man's left sleeve. The right sleeve is slit vertically, revealing its fur lining, and then buttoned shut; this too is mysterious. As it does not reveal the *chemise*, it cannot be the sleeve of the *pourpoint*, yet the sleeves of the *robe* are still full at this date, not tight as here. Above the collar of the *pourpoint* peeps a tiny section of the *chemise*. The padding in a doublet could save a man's life, as John Paston I discovered in 1461 when he was stabbed twice with a dagger, but saved by his doublet.

**101 Barbara Vetzer and her daughter, 1467**
Friedrich Walther

**Note** This shows the differences in outdoor dress
for married women and unmarried girls in
Nördlingen in southern Germany.

**Head** The mother wears a linen undercap with a
veil over her chin and another, heavily starched
one on top of her cap, which then is tucked under
the chin. The daughter's hair is uncovered and is
dressed in plaits at the sides of the head with a
fringe at the back, and a jewelled band round her
head.

**Body** The mother's pleated and high-waisted
gown is well hidden under her fur-lined cloak; the
fur has the black tails of ermine, but is not white as
ermine is. The daughter wears a doublet-like
undergarment with tight sleeves and laced collar,
under a gown whose sleeves serve both as hanging
sleeves and cloak. Its 'waistline' is immediately
below the bust.

**102 Bertha, Duchess of Burgundy,
supervising the building of the church of the
Magdalene, Vezelay, c.1465**
Loyset Liedet

**Head** The Duchess wears modestly horned veils,
perhaps because she is clearly intending to spend a
considerable time out of doors. The workmen vary
in their ability or desire to wear fashionable head
gear.

**Body** The Duchess's *robe* with its trailing skirts
has to be gathered up to allow her to walk, and
thus reveals that even someone of her wealth has to
think about attaching a removable hem to her *cote*.
Some of the workmen wear simple *robes* and
aprons, while others prefer to work in their
*pourpoints*, sometimes with their hose let down to
their knees, revealing their drawers.

**103 Gerard de Roussillon and his wife Berthe are presented by the Queen of France to Charles the Bald, c.1466–7**
Loyset Liedet

**Note** The King's attire is deliberately shown as archaic.

**Head** The courtiers wear a variety of hats, the most noticeable being the very tall caps deriving from the acorn-cup cap. The caps of the Queen and her lady are likewise intent on growing upwards, and are draped in long, fine veils which form a small 'gable' at the front. Berthe, having shared her husband's disgrace and exile, wears a more modest cap, in keeping with her position.

**Body** The King's bodyguard wear breastplates over very short *pourpoints* with puffed upper sleeves; the courtiers wear similar *pourpoints* under their short capes or their *robes*, which are pleated only at the points of the shoulder. The Queen has the most scooped, and hence the most fashionable, neckline. Her cuffs cover her hands, but the cuffs of the less fashionable Berthe stop at the wrists. Gerard shares his wife's neglect of high fashion: his *robe* belongs to the period of his greater favour, represented here by the style of *c*.1440.

**104 William Gybbys and his wives Alice,
Margaret and Marion, c.1470(?)**
Anon. English engraver

**Note** Gybbys died in 1485, but the dress does not
tally with this date. The wives' outfits are almost
identical and are presumably from a standard
pattern: their sleeves suggest a date c.1450, and
the bodices perhaps c.1460. Gybbys's appearance
belongs c.1470.

**Head** Gybbys wears his hair cut in a fringe and
over his ears.

**Body** Gybbys's gown has the diminishing
pleating of the years around 1470, and the
concomitant levelling of the shoulder-line. The
gown, however, retains the draw-in waist at this
date, and it is ankle-length because of the
formality of the situation.

**105  A woman of the Hofer family, c.1470**
Swabian School

**Note**  This portrait shows very clearly the
continuing 'masculine' look in women's dress in
Germany. The fly which appears to rest on the
headdress is in fact a piece of *trompe l'oeil*, with the
fly 'resting' on the surface of the picture.

**Head**  The hair is completely hidden by a wasp's
nest-shaped headdress composed of numerous
veils with tiny fluted edges, set to overlap like roof
tiles, and held together by several pins along the
top layer of 'tiles'. The final veil is treated like the
shoulder-cape and tippet of a man's hood.

**Body**  The gown is trimmed at its cuffs and high
neckline with white fur. Underneath is a garment
with a damask(?) collar like that of a man's
doublet, held in position by lacing.

**Accessories**  A pendant and rings. The sprig of
forget-me-not makes it probable that this was a
betrothal or wedding portrait.

**106  Portrait of an older woman, c.1470**
Hans Memlinc

**Note**  This portrait shows the principles of greater modesty and lesser
extravagance which governed the dress of older women.

**Head**  A small dark truncated steeple headdress is covered in a double
thickness of veiling heavy enough to hide the eyebrows and ears when it is
drawn down over the (presumably) wrinkled brow.

**Body**  Although the *robe* follows the generally prevailing fashion for a
scooped neckline with wide fur collar, high-set waistline, and narrow sleeves
extending to the knuckles, the neckline covers more of the shoulders, the
black *pièce* is worn higher, and the scarf (pinned together at the front) is
somewhat thicker than in younger women's fashions.

**Accessories**  Jewellery is limited to a ring on the forefinger. There is a belt,
worn high.

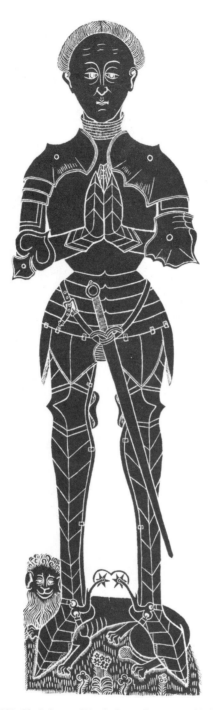

**107 Sir John and Lady Joan Curzon, c.1472**
Anon. English engraver

**Note** Sir John's armour is spiky enough for a date *c*.1470, although his hair is very short. His wife's dress is also consistent with this date.

**Head** Lady Curzon wears a lozenge-patterned pill-box cap at the back of her head, with a short veil drawn back from the forehead into small 'wings'.

**Body** The cords of the fur-lined cloak obscure most of the details of the neckline, but it appears the breasts are pushed up by the very tight bodice. The 'waist' is high and narrow, and the skirt flares from the hips.

**108 Robert Ingylton and his wives Margaret Dymoke, Clemens Cantilupe and Isabel Lester, and their children, c.1472**
Anon. English engraver

**Note** Ingylton died in 1472, and although his hairstyle and those of his sons are rather too short to be fashionable at that date, the rest of the dress and the armour fit that date.

**Head** The mothers and daughters wear different headdresses, the mothers' being the more old-fashioned short veils over small under-structures whose horns are drawing together, while the daughters' are the more fashionable large pill-box caps on the backs of their heads, under 'butterfly' veils.

**Body** The sons wear full-length gowns with fashionably wide, straight shoulders, still drawn in at the waist to emphasize the bulk above. The women all wear gowns with wide, curved necklines, unnaturally narrow bodices, and turned-back cuffs, but the daughters' gowns are more fashionable in that they flare from the hips, not from the waist.

**109 Jan de Witte, aged 30, 1473**
Bruges Master of 1473

**Note** This and the following portrait, of de Witte's wife, probably commemorate their marriage, and they appear to be in their finest clothes.

**Head** The hair is roughly cut in the fashionable 'page boy' style.

**Body** This *robe*, of grey damask, is in keeping with the growing taste for blacks, greys and browns. The extreme length of its sleeves suggests that it is not an everyday garment, as does the careful display of as much of its 'skirt' as possible as it swirls around him on the ground.

**Accessories** There is a fine gold chain worn round the *pourpoint* collar, and a ring is worn near the top of the fourth finger of the left hand. The *cornette* is retained to carry a shaggy tall-crowned hat with a small brim.

**110 Maria Hoose, aged 17, 1473**
Bruges Master of 1473

**Note** Her coat of arms, impaled with that of her husband, contains a punning reference to her name: three baggy hose.

**Head** The hairline is unnaturally high, suggesting plucking of the forehead; and the slanting of the eyes and eyebrows suggests that the hair is pulled back uncomfortably tightly before being confined in the small cap, which is embroidered with thistles. The loop on the forehead is unusually large, and the fine veil is drawn up over the forehead into a 'gable', which is pinned to the cap. Such headdresses become more usual in the early 1480s.

**Body** This velvet *robe* appears to have been designed to inflict the maximum discomfort on its wearer, as it demands a tiny circular waist and impossibly thin arms. The bust is compressed by a red *pièce*, which picks up the red of the necklace's stones.

## 111  Margaret of Denmark, Queen of James III of Scotland, with St George, 1473–8
Hugo van der Goes

**Note**  Although this shows the Queen in her ceremonial robe, which is meant to be relatively free of fashionable features, and hence more dignified, it is still datable to the 1470s.

**Head**  The headdress is a 'frozen' form of the horned and netted headdress, now reserved for ceremonial wear, covered in pearls, some of which would move with the wearer's movements. It is topped by a sort of crown. The loop on the forehead places it in the years when such devices were made necessary by fashionable headdresses.

**Body**  The blue-black cloak and open supertunic with their ermine lining are datable to the 1470s by the way in which the tooled leather(?) Y–shaped front section creates the V-shaped neckline of the 1470s, with a *pièce* beneath. The red cloth of gold kirtle was originally painted with much narrower sleeves, another hallmark of the early years of the decade.

**Accessories**  The Queen's collar is typical of those of the 1470s, and Van de Goes used a version of it in 'The Portinari Altarpiece', which is also datable *c*.1473–8. Among her jewels the Queen did have 'a collere of rubeis set with threis of perle', with a pendant, a diamond and a large pearl.

**112 Sophia von Bylant with St James the Greater, 1475**
The Master of the St Bartholomew Altarpiece

**Note** Sophia von Bylant was widowed *c*.1459, but she is not shown as a widow. She lived in an area now on the Dutch-German border and her dress is like that worn in Cologne.

**Head** The headdress is a more ponderous version of the Franco-Flemish steeple headdress with a shorter veil.

**Body** The gown, of velvet cloth of gold, has the narrow sleeves and fur cuffs fashionable in Flanders, but also has the bunch of folds beneath the bust which was fashionable in the Cologne area. The wide neckline with minimal trimming and *pièce* is typical of much German dress, and in some areas became so indecent that it was discouraged by law: in 1480 girls in Nuremberg were ordered to wear necklines no lower than two finger-breadths under the points of their collarbones.

**113 Unknown young man at prayer, c.1475**
Hans Memlinc

**Head** The 'page boy' haircut is growing longer at the back.

**Body** This extremely tight and skimpy black *robe* (or coat?) is worn over an equally skimpy red velvet *pourpoint*, which has black laces across the front. The armhole seams are no longer sewn shut all the way round, and the *chemise* shows through the openings at the tops of the sleeves. This move to tightness in men's dress is very rapid in the 1470s and is a most remarkable reversal of aesthetic values in such a short time. Perhaps it was the basis of the remarks addressed to Edward IV in 1475 in *The Boke of Noblesse*, where it was pointed out to the King that the French had abandoned the extravangance in dress which had ruined many of the poor in England.

**114 Sir John Donne, c.1477**
Hans Memlinc
See colour plate between pp. 96 and 97.

**115 Lady Donne and her daughter**
Hans Memlinc
See colour plate between pp. 96 and 97.

**116 One of the two wives of (?) John Carent of Silton, late 1470s**
Anon. English sculptor

**Note** John Carent died in 1478, a date consistent with the design of the necklace worn by this woman.

**Head** This headdress is a curious, but by no means unique, combination of large cauls, vestiges of 'butterfly' veils, and a deep frontlet. The 'butterfly' headdresses seem to have been consistently (and not surprisingly) beyond the powers of sculptors to represent, which would explain their truncated appearance on effigies. The frontlet in France or Flanders would have been narrower and allowed to fall more naturally on to the shoulders, as in plate 115.

**Body** The lady wears the ceremonial robe.

**Accessories** The necklace retains its collar-like shape, but the harshness of the old outline is broken by pendent droplets at the lower edge.

**117 The widow and family of Sir Thomas Urswyck, Recorder of London and Chief Baron of the Exchequer, c.1479**
Anon. English engraver

**Note** Sir Thomas died in 1479 and the dress suggests the brass was ordered shortly after his death.

**Head** The widow wears the plain heavy veil and wimple of widowhood; her daughters wear 'butterfly' veils held out on wires over pill-box caps set on the back of the head, or, if unmarried, truncated steeple-shaped caps over flowing hair.

**Body** The man's gown on the left is fashionably tight, with tiny lapels. The widow is enveloped in a cloak and a loose gown with wide sleeves. The daughters' gowns have the new squarer neckline, with the breasts pushed up and just kept decent by the stomacher. The return to visibility of the centre front closing of the gown, and the loss of the deep belt, are other new features, now gaining general acceptance.

**118 An unknown lady, sometimes called Alice Neville, late 1470s(?)**
Anon. English sculptor

**Note** This effigy conveys very well the tightness of fashionable sleeves.

**Head** The hair is completely concealed within a headdress which pays no more than lip-service to its origins in a proper net, and on top is a scrap of veiling, forming narrow ridges along the top of the head.

**Body** The gown is typical of high fashion in England in the 1470s with its wide, scooped neckline, tight knuckle-length sleeves, and skirt which flares from the hips.

**Accessories** A narrow belt, with circular clasps and a pomander(?) on a chain, is worn at natural waist level, forecasting a shift in the perception of the position of the waist, from the designer's point of view.

110

**119 Unknown young man, c.1480**
The Master of the View of Sainte Gudule

**Note** This picture must show fashion in Brussels, as the church in the background is that of Notre Dame du Sablon in Brussels.

**Head** The bonnet is a truncated version of the tall caps of the 1460s, with a small 'brim' tapering from back to front.

**Body** The *robe* is a stark contrast of black and white, in keeping with the prevailing taste for such combinations. The 'lapel' is not yet properly formed or worried about, as what is probably the *cornette* flattens the right 'lapel' as it crosses the body. The slit in the robe sleeve is a very pronounced example of this recently introduced feature. The mid-brown (*tanné?*) *pourpoint* is tied shut by laces with metal tips, and its sleeves are becoming slightly baggy.

**120 Henry Stathum, his wives Anne Bothe, Elizabeth Seyntlow and his widow Margaret Stanhop, c.1481**
Anon. English engraver

**Note** This brass is probably datable to the time of Henry's death in 1481 and is interesting because it shows an attempt to portray the two wives who predeceased him in by now old-fashioned dress, such as they might have worn in their lifetimes. The availability of such images to the brass engraver could well explain why so many brasses refuse to fit neatly into a logical sequence of changes in fashion.

**Head** The widow wears a long veil and pleated wimple while the wives wear the headdresses of the 1440s.

**Body** The wives' gowns are marked as old-fashioned by their baggy sleeves and loose cuffs. Although widows were not really meant to observe fashion, and her gown has the less fashionable belted waistline, the widow has been unable to avoid the long mitten-like cuffs of fashionable dress, here turned back to show the praying gesture of her hands.

**121 Sir Ralph Fitzherbert and his wife Elizabeth Marshall, c.1483**
Anon. English sculptor

**Note** Sir Ralph died in 1483 and it would have been impolitic, not to say impossible, to display the Yorkist collar, as he does, after the accession of Henry VII in 1485.

**Head** Sir Ralph, not being a very young man, wears his hair slightly shorter than is fashionable. His wife's headdress is the standard sculptor's response to the horned or 'butterfly' headdress.

**Body** Lady Elizabeth's ceremonial robe shows the form which is quite common in the last quarter of the fifteenth century, with what often appears to be a shortened sideless supertunic, whose hem is, as here, apparently turned to the outside – or simply marked by a band of fur at mid-calf height.

**122 Female weepers from the Fitzherbert tomb, c.1483**
Anon. English sculptor

**Head** The two women wear headdresses like that of Lady Fitzherbert; the girl wears her hair loose.

**Body** All three figures wear gowns with tight sleeves and bodices, although the girl has an open laced front to her bodice, and wears her cuffs over her hands, while the woman beside her has turned her cuffs back. The third woman has a most unusual torso shape, more late Victorian in its hourglass appearance than the usual slender late Gothic woman.

**123 Male weepers from the Fitzherbert
tomb, c.1483**
Anon. English sculptor

**Head**  The hair is worn at a variety of lengths at
and below the ears.

**Body**  Little cloth is still being used in the gowns,
but the feeling of breath-stopping tightness is
going. One sleeve retains vertical slits at the top.
Underneath are doubléts with square-fronted
collars and aggressively pronounced lacing across
the chest.

**124 Sir Thomas Peyton and his two wives, both called Margaret, c.1484**
Anon. English engraver

**Note** The necklines are consistent with the date of Sir Thomas's death, 1484, despite the shortness of his hair.

**Head** Both women wear fully developed 'butterfly' headdresses.

**Body** The necklines of the gowns show a peculiarly English feature at this date, the upward point of the collar and the stomacher at the cleavage. It is increasingly usual to turn back the cuffs, though the retention of the belt under the bust is slightly old-fashioned. The gown on the left is remarkable for its textile, which is in a standard cloth of gold pattern, and instead of having the more usual fur collar, cuffs and hem of the other gown, these areas are made of another patterned textile, perhaps figured velvet.

**Accessories** Both women have necklaces composed of a series of large leaf shapes, such as came into fashion c.1480.

### 125 Ralph Nevill, Earl of Westmorland, and Elizabeth Percy, c.1484
Anon. English sculptor

**Note** The Countess died in 1436 and the Earl in 1484, but features of her dress suggest that the figures were carved about the time of his death rather than hers.

**Head** The Countess wears a truncated steeple headdress with a narrow frontlet, which is unusual in England but acceptable in Flanders until *c.*1480.

**Body** Although her outfit is the ceremonial robe, the Countess has the immodest neckline which appears on some brasses *c.*1480, and the skirt of her sideless supertunic is 'divided' horizontally below the hips.

### 126 Unknown man, his wife and his mother, 1486
The Master of the Legend of St Ursula

**Note** This painting shows the variety of dress worn by a middle-class Bruges family: the mother is 62, her son 30 and his wife 23.

**Head** The man's hair is too short to be fashionable. His mother, as an older and presumably widowed woman, wears a thick linen veil pulled down over her forehead and tucked together at the back of the head, while his wife, as a much younger woman, is permitted to show a little of her hair and all of her forehead under a semi-transparent veil which floats freely at the sides.

**Body** The man's *robe* is still worn closed, though it is not cut full. The women's *robes* are very similar, except in the dark colouring of that of the mother and in the way she has filled in the neckline with a solid shoulder-cape(?) which is pinned shut at the top. The wife has the usual arrangement of *pièce* and linen scarf, with the addition at the sides of what is perhaps an early instance of the *brassière*.

**127 Martin van Nieuwenhove, aged 23, 1487**
Hans Memlinc

**Note** This is the dress of a young Bruges patrician, and therefore probably the height of fashion.

**Head** The hair is fluffy and reaches the shoulders.

**Body** Here we see the start of new arrangements in the layers of men's dress: the *robe*, with its wide lapels, sits out on the shoulders and has vertical slits in its sleeves, through which appear the arms in the two-part *pourpoint* sleeves. The lower sleeves are of velvet while the upper sleeves, which are more rarely seen, are of a cheaper material. The same velvet is used across the chest, but may be only a large *pièce*, over which is tied the body of the *pourpoint* (or is it a coat?), made of the cheaper material used in the upper sleeves of the *pourpoint*.

**128 The De Waele family, late 1470s(?)**
Anon. Brussels Painter

**Head** The men's hair is generally clear of their collars. The mother and daughter wear chin cloths whose depths are regulated by their ages, as are the opacity of their veils; the daughter's veil shows that she is wearing a small cap under it.

**Body** The men have simply-shaped *robes*, with rather too-long sleeves; the lapels, such as they are, are more marked on the *robes* of the men on the left. The *robes* of the mother and daughter present a strange contrast, with the mother hanging on to the V-neckline and baggy sleeves of her youth, while her daughter has adopted the newest fashion, a *robe* with a square neckline which is emphasized by a narrow fur edging, which also marks the front closing. Both women seem to wear black *brassières* under their robes.

**129 John Barton and his wife, c.1491**
Anon. English sculptor

**Note** Barton came from Lancashire to Nottinghamshire and became rich through the wool trade with France. There is clearly an attempt being made to produce portraits of this elderly couple, which, to judge by Barton's hairstyle, must have been carved about the time of his death in 1491, yet otherwise show remarkable conservatism in their dress.

**Head** Barton's hairstyle would not disgrace a fashion-conscious middle-class youth c.1490. His wife wears one of the very solid-looking, vertical frontlets that are sometimes found in the 1490s.

**Body** Barton's gown, with its closed front, trace of a collar and token observance of pleating in the body, is about twenty years out of date. Approximately the same time lag can be seen in his wife's gown. She has filled in the neckline as her age demands.

**Accessories** Barton carries a purse on his narrow belt; his wife marks her unfashionably high waistline by a broader belt.

119

**130  A donor with St Clement,**
**c.1485–90(?)**
Style of Simon
Marmion

**Note**  This and the
following picture, of
the man's wife,
together present
interesting questions
about the speed of total
acceptance of new
fashions.

**Head**  The length of
the hair is suitable for a
well-to-do sitter, past
his first youth *c*.1485.

**Body**  The *robe*, with
its slit upper sleeve and
only slightly rolled-
back 'lapel', suggests a
date in the later 1470s
or very early 1480s, yet
the covering of the
*chemise* front points
firmly to the 1480s.

**131 A donatrix with St Elizabeth of Hungary, c.1485–90(?)**
Style of Simon Marmion

**Head** The steeple headdress has been considerably shortened, as it was by about 1480, and is covered by a small transparent veil which is drawn down to the eyebrows. On top is another veil, folded double and ironed to produce a heart-shaped frontlet. This harks back to the frontlets of the 1470s, and looks forward to the starched caps of the 1490s.

**Body** The *robe* has a fully developed square neckline, with a *brassière* beneath, and a waistline near natural waist level. The cuffs are now being drawn back on themselves, as will become much more common in the early 1490s. The *robe* is more fashionable than the headdress.

**Accessories** Rings, a necklace of two rows of interlinked rings, and a narrow but shiny belt to draw attention to the new waistline.

121

**132 William van Overbeke with St William, c.1485–90**
Anon. Flemish painter

**Head** The hair is curled at the neck.

**Body** The *robe* has fashionably over-long sleeves and fur-trimmed 'lapels' which stand up. Underneath is a garment which hides all but a tiny strip of the *chemise*-neck.

**Accessories** Over the right shoulder hangs a *cornette* which probably supports a hat at the back.

**133 Johanna de Keysert, wife of Willem van Overbeke, with St John the Baptist, c.1485–90**
Anon. Flemish painter

**Head** A small cap, derived from the steeple cap, with a large front loop, sits above what must be a plucked or shaven forehead.

**Body** The *robe* is of the new pattern, with square neck and obvious centre front fastening, here closed with buttons, and the waist at its natural level. The cuffs are now three layers thick and are widening. Beneath the gown is a black *brassière*.

**Accessories** An elaborately knotted and twisted belt is the only touch of extravagance in this very plain outfit.

**134 Woman at the Antwerp Archers' Feast, c.1491–3**
The Master of Frankfurt

**Note** This woman is of the middle classes.

**Head** The veil with its central fold is worn over a small cap set at the back of the head.

**Body** The *robe* shows itself to be slightly behind high fashion with the upward pointing of the lower edge of the neckline, and the simply turned back cuffs. The skirt has, however, the fashionable train, which is bunched up at the side. Some women developed a swayback stance in the 1490s, as we see here.

**135 George Crane, c.1491**
Anon. English sculptor

**Note** This effigy is almost certainly datable to George's death in 1491, since children would not think of ordering their own effigies.

**Head** The hair is of a fashionable length and shagginess.

**Body** The gown, with its straight lapels, is worn open across the chest to reveal a coat with tapering lapels and a stomacher(?). This combination of gown, coat and stomacher(?) becomes the norm in the 1490s.

**Accessories** A cap with a shallow crown and a narrow brim is attached to a tippet which runs down the body to below the knees.

**136 The Lover greets the God of Love, early 1490s**
Anon. Flemish illuminator

**Note** This manuscript is made particularly interesting by the attempts of the illuminator to produce old-fashioned dress for the Lover, whom he dresses, as here, in fringing to suggest the dagging of the start of the century, and to whom he gives a belt with pendent pieces of metalwork, also derived from the earlier period: the *Roman de la Rose* was now a venerable classic and as such worthy of some historical research in dress.

**Head** Both men have fashionably long hair, with the God wearing a flat cap with turned-up side flaps.

**Body** The God has a very loose *robe* with long tubular sleeves, slit to allow the arms through at a convenient height. It is lined and trimmed with velvet at the lapels and 'cuff', and is pulled across the body in the fashionably casual manner. Beneath he has a velvet garment which completely hides the *chemise*.

**Accessories** The God's shoes have the new rounded toes; the Lover's right shoe has an old-fashioned pointed toe, but the artist seems to have failed to remember this 'historical' detail and has given the left shoe a rounded toe.

126

**137 A young couple praying before the Virgin and Child, early 1490s**
The Master of 1499

**Note** This Flemish couple are well-to-do, but not aristocratic, to judge by the wife's linen headdress.

**Head** The man's hairstyle is reasonably fashionable. His wife's thick linen veil has an ironed-in dip at the top of the head, and it is tucked under itself at the back to neaten the outline.

**Body** The man's *robe*, with its spotted fur (lynx?) lapels and cuffs, exemplifies the extravagant display of surface pattern encouraged by these increasingly important areas. Beneath he wears a *cote* with tiny lapels, and a dark, gathered inner garment, as yet unidentified. His wife's *robe* has the usual front fastening, almost square neckline and *brassière* beneath. The cuffs are the most interesting part, as they are beginning to be drawn away from their fur lining, so that the textile of the dress is gathered in behind the fur and more of the fur is brought out.

**138 Pierre, duc de Bourbon, with St Peter, c.1493**
The Master of Moulins

**Note** This is French fashion at the highest social level.

**Head** The Duke tries to wear his thinning hair in the fashionable style. His cap, with its soft brim tied round it, is a descendant of the tall caps of the 1460s.

**Body** The *robe* is made of a rich red velvet which seems to have been shot through with black; this is a fairly common method of dulling red velvets up to the 1530s. It is lined and trimmed with a thick, soft brown fur, which appears at the back of the right sleeve, showing that sleeve and armhole seams are not always completely closed. Underneath is a black inner garment.

**Accessories** A collar of knots and cockle shells, of the Order of St Michael, seen slaying the dragon on the pendant.

**139 Anne de Beaujeu, duchesse de Bourbon, and daughter of Louis XI of France, with St John the Evangelist, c.1493**
The Master of Moulins

**Head** Only a trace of the stiff caps of earlier years remains under the black veil, which is worn far enough back to reveal a finely pleated gauze coif, edged with crimped gold ribbon(?)

**Body** The *robe* with its V-shaped neckline and slight sense of a sway-back stance is apparently typical of French women's dress in the early 1490s. The cuffs are widening and displaying their ermine lining as well as their ermine binding where the lining meets the velvet outer layer.

**Accessories** An unusual belt-like arrangement of pearls and gems mounted in gold is suspended from a lace round the neck.

**140 Suzanne de Bourbon, aged about two, c.1493**
The Master of Moulins

**Note** It may have been usual to dress babies and young children in white: Suzanne is shown here in white, and her cousin the Dauphin was always dressed in white when he was a baby.

**Head** A box-shaped damask bonnet is worn over a coif which is tied under the chin. There is a vague resemblance to adult dress in the flap of cloth which extends on to the shoulders.

**Body** The *robe*, of damask, has sleeves like Suzanne's mother's, but its bodice is treated differently: it either has a square neckline and closes at the child's left side, or it has a V-shaped neckline, partly obscured by a bib in front. In either case, the result is that the child has an element of squareness to her neckline which her mother has yet to adopt.

**141 Philip the Fair, c.1493–5**
Netherlandish school

**Note** This and the next plate show two of the most important children of their day, the offspring of Mary, heiress of the Dukes of Burgundy, and the future Emperor Maximilian I. The richness of their dress reflects this importance.

**Head** Philip wears a black cap with turned-up sides on his fluffy shoulder-length hair; men must have washed their hair every day to achieve this effect.

**Body** The *robe* of cloth of gold has ermine-covered lapels, and the vertical slash in the upper sleeve is just beginning at the bottom of the picture. Beneath is the mysterious all-concealing inner garment.

**Accessories** A collar of the Order of the Golden Fleece.

142 Margaret of Austria, c.1493–5
Netherlandish school

**142 Margaret of Austria, c.1493–5**
Netherlandish school

**Head** Margaret's black head-covering is decorated along its front edge, and is turned back on top of the head to reveal its paler lining; from this will develop the 'French hood' of the sixteenth century.

**Body** Margaret's *robe* of cloth of gold has a slight upwards curve to the lower edge of the neckline, yet another means of avoiding commitment to a truly squared-off neckline; the reluctance to accept such a neckline is quite marked in the 1490s. The *brassière* is worn more open than it is by the middle classes.

**Accessories** A pendant on a lace and a fashionable necklace of flat links.

**143 The King of France(?) with St Giles and the hind, c.1495–1500**
The Master of St Giles
See colour plate between pp. 96 and 97.

131

**144 Jean, Comte de la Tour d'Auvergne, with St John the Baptist, 1495–98**
The Master of the de la Tour d'Auvergne Triptych

**Head** The hair is of fashionable length and texture.

**Body** The outer layer is a red garment which has the lapels and vertical armhole slit of a *robe*, but the shape of a cloak which is at least semi-circular. Underneath is a cloth of gold *cote*(?) with baggy upper sleeves and more fitted lower sleeves.

**Accessories** High-fronted shoes with bulbous toes, and stockings or tights in two layers: a dark, inner one and a paler outer layer which is cut into narrow vertical strips for most of its length.

**145 Jeanne de Bourbon-Vendôme, Comtesse de la Tour d'Auvergne, 1495–98**
The Master of the de la Tour d'Auvergne Triptych

**Head** The development of the French hood continues apace, with the black outer layer moved farther back on the head to reveal two bands of crimped gauze on the front of the under-cap; the black cloth falls on to the shoulders while the inner cap stops at the base of the throat.

**Body** The cloth of gold *robe* has the new side fastening at the Comtesse's right side, and the sleeves have very rapidly developed into huge funnel shapes which have to be turned back to near the elbows if the hands are to be used. The *pièce* has a fairly wide neckline, and under it is still worn a linen scarf.

**Accessories** A collar of enamelled(?) flowers at the base of the neck, and a large cruciform pendant with pendant pearls is suspended from a chain.

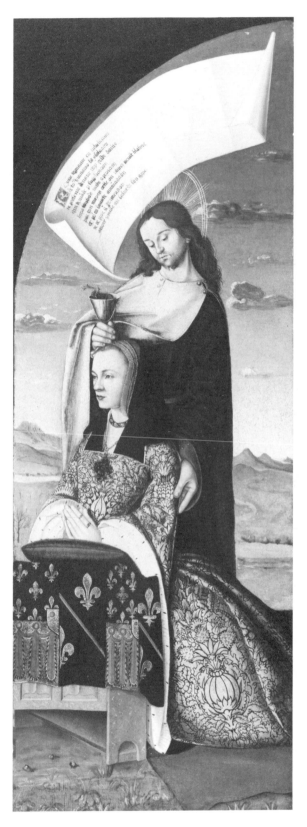

**146 An unknown Flemish couple, c.1495–1500**
The Master of the Embroidered Foliage

**Note** The sobriety of the dress suggests that this couple are middle class.

**Head** The man struggles to wear his hair fashionably. Although the woman has the dark, shoulder-length veil most commonly worn by aristocratic women, her use of the heart-shaped under-cap suggest she is really middle class.

**Body** Although the man has pronounced lapels on his *robe*, his wide cuffs are not yet turned back. His wife's *robe* is of the usual middle-class pattern for the 1490s, with sleeves which are widening quite markedly at the cuffs. Her *brassière* is drawn firmly over her upper chest.

**Accessories** Both sitters have rings and large chains as jewellery, the method of joining the links of the wife's chain being quite intricate. She also has a narrow belt with a small buckle and a shield-shaped metalwork end.

**147 Hermann Rinck, mayor of Cologne, and his wife Gertrud von Ballem, datable 1489–96; perhaps c.1495**
The Master of the Aachen Altarpiece

**Note** This painting shows how the dress of men in Cologne was very like that worn elsewhere, and how the dress of women in Cologne maintained only partial contact with the dress of women in Flanders.

**Head** The young men in the background have hairstyles and hats which could be seen in contemporary France or Flanders, but Gertrud's retention of a steeple-shaped headdress would immediately mark her as foreign.

**Body** The young men's gowns are modest versions of high fashion, while Rinck's *mi-parti* gown is presumably a livery of a guild or the town council. Gertrud's gown sleeves would not be remarked on by her Flemish neighbours, but the bodice of her gown, with its rounded neckline and off-the-shoulder effect, are very German.

**149 John Clerk and his wife Lucy, c.1497**
Anon. English engraver

**148 An unknown woman of Cologne,
c.1495–1500** (opposite)
Cologne school

**Head** The truncated steeple cap sits at the back of
the head and has a small dark frontlet, as well as a
very fine gauze heart-shaped frontlet. The hair
hangs down behind.

**Body** The gown has the usual German scooped
neckline and pleats which begin at the bust.
Although the underpieces seem to give the outfit a
square neckline, that is not really their purpose in
German design: where a woman does have a low
neckline filled in with a horizontal band, the band
is always much more decorative than the Franco-
Flemish *pièce*, and the amount of embroidery
which is sometimes lavished on it suggests that it
was as a potential means of display, and not as a
means to achieving a square neckline, that it was
prized.

**Note** This and plate 150 suggest that the
English middle classes were very slow to pick up
all the changes which had been taking place in
dress across the Channel. John Clerk died in 1497,
which must be presumed to be the approximate
date of the brass.

**Head** John's hairstyle is unremarkable, and
Lucy's veil is very old-fashioned.

**Body** Only the expanding sleeves of John's
carefully closed gown give any hint of the trends of
the 1490s. Lucy's gown has a properly squared
neckline and the lowered waistline, but her tight
sleeves with their flipped-back cuffs are hopelessly
out of date by Continental standards.

**Accessories** John carries a fashionably flat cap on
a tippet, over his left shoulder, and a purse hangs
at the belt, which also supports a rosary.

**150 Robert Serche and his wife Anne, c.1502**
Anon. English engraver

**Note** Although this brass does not strictly
speaking belong to the fifteenth century (Robert
died in January 1501 [1502 new style]), it is
included to emphasize the conservatism of
Englishwomen's dress.

**Head** The most important feature is Anne's
headdress, which is an early version of the 'gable'
headdress worn by English women into the 1530s

and sometimes later. It is split vertically at the
shoulders into a frontlet and a longer veil at the back.

**Body** Robert's gown with its furry lapels and
cuffs is moderately fashionable, but Anne still
refuses to adopt the wide sleeves or the square
neckline, preferring instead to split her cuffs and
turn them back, and to force her neckline up in an
inverted V above the centre-front closing.

**Accessories** Anne has a very long, loosely
buckled belt.

# Select Bibliography

## BOOKS AND ARTICLES ON DRESS

**Note** The division between this and the next section of the bibliography is based on the interests of the writers: in this section are works by people writing as dress historians, and in the next are works and transcripts by people primarily interested in history or literature.

Evans, J., *Dress in Medieaval France*, Oxford, 1952

Hawkins, C., 'A fifteenth century pattern for 'chausses'', *Costume*, no. 6, 1972, pp. 84–5

Nevinson, J., 'Buttons and Buttonholes in the Fourteenth Century', *Costume*, No. 11, 1977, pp. 38–44

Newton, S.M., *Fashion in the Age of the Black Prince: A Study of the Years 1340–1365*, Woodbridge, 1980

Scott, M., *Late Gothic Europe, 1400–1500*, The History of Dress Series, London, 1980

Staniland, K., 'The Medieval 'Corset'', *Costume*, no. 3, 1969, pp. 10–13

Staniland, K., 'Clothing and Textiles at the Court of Edward III 1342–1352', *Collectanea Londiniensia: Studies in London archaeology and history presented to Ralph Merrifield*, London and Middlesex Archaeological Society Special Paper No. 2, 1978

Sutton, A., and Hammond, P.W., (ed.), *The Coronation of Richard III: the Extant Documents*, Gloucester, 1983

## BOOKS AND ARTICLES CONTAINING USEFUL INFORMATION ON DRESS

Amyot, T., 'Letter from Thomas Amyot, Esq. F.R.S. Treasurer, to the Earl of Aberdeen, K.T. President, accompanying a transcript of two Rolls, containing an Inventory of Effects formerly belonging to Sir John Fastolfe', *Archaeologia* XXI, pp. 232–80, London, 1827

Baildon, W.P., 'Wardrobe Account of 16–17 Richard II, 1393–4', *Archaeologia*, LXII, pp. 497–514, London, 1911

Baildon, W.P., 'The Trousseau of Princess Philippa, wife of Eric, King of Denmark, Norway, and Sweden', *Archaeologia*, LXVII, pp. 163–88, London, 1916

Baldwin, F.E., *Sumptuary Legislation and Personal Regulation in England*, Johns Hopkins University Studies in Historical and Political Science, series 44, no. 1, Baltimore, 1926

Birdsall, J. (trans.), and Newhall, R.A. (ed.), *The Chronicle of Jean de Venette*, New York, 1953

Chichester, The Earl of, 'Copy of an Inventory of Queen Katherine's Wardrobe', *Sussex Archaeological Collections*, XXXVII, pp. 173–6, London, 1890

Collier, J.P. (ed.), *Household Books of John Duke of Norfolk and Thomas Earl of Surrey Temp. 1481–1490*, Roxburghe Club, London, 1844

Davis, N. (ed.), *The Paston Letters A Selection in Modern Spelling*, Oxford, 1983

Dickson, T., *Compota Thesaurariorum Regum Scotorum. Accounts of the Lord High Treasurer of Scotland*, Edinburgh, I, 1877

Harvey, J.H., 'The Wilton Diptych. A Re-examination', *Archaeologia*, XCVIII, pp. 1–28, London, 1961

Haydon, F.S. (ed.), *Eulogium (Historiarum sive Temporis): Chronicon ab orbe condito usque ad annum Domini M.CCC.LXV., a monacho quodam Malmesburiensi exaratum*, 3 vols., Rolls Series, 9, London, 1858–63

de Laborde, Comte, *Les Ducs de Bourgogne*, Seconde partie, *Preuves*, 3 vols., Paris, 1849–52

Myers, A.R., 'The captivity of a royal witch: the household accounts of Queen Joan of Navarre, 1419–21', *Bulletin of the John Rylands Library*, XXIV, pp. 263–84, Manchester, 1940; and XXVI, pp. 82–100, Manchester, 1942

Myers, A.R., 'The jewels of Queen Margaret of Anjou', *Bulletin of the John Rylands Library*, XLII, pp. 113–31, Manchester, 1960'

Nichols, J., *Collection of all the Wills now known to be extant of the Kings and Queens of England*, etc., London, 1780

Nichols, J.G., 'On collars of the royal livery', *The Gentleman's Magazine*, CXII, pp. 157–61, 250–8, 378–80, 477–85, London, 1842

Nichols, J.G., 'Observations on the Heraldic Devices discovered on the Effigies of Richard the Second and his Queen in Westminster Abbey', etc., *Archaeologia*, XXIX, pp. 32–59, London, 1842

Nicolas, N.H., *Testamenta Vetusta*, 2 vols., London, 1826

Nicolas, N.H., *Privy Purse Expenses of Elizabeth of York: Wardrobe Accounts of Edward the Fourth*, London, 1830

Nicolas, N.H., 'Observations on the Institution of the Most Noble Order of the Garter', *Archaeologia*, XXXI, pp. 1–163, London, 1856

Occleve, Thomas (ed. T. Wright), *De Regimine Principum*, Roxburghe Club, London, 1860

Picot, G., *La Farce de Maistre Pathelin*, Paris, 1972

Robinson, F.N. (ed.), *The Complete Works of Geoffrey Chaucer*, 2nd edition, Oxford, 1974

Safford, E.W., 'An Account of the Expenses of Eleanor, sister of Edward III, on the occasion of her marriage to Reynald, Count of Guelders', *Archaeologia*, LXXVII, pp. 111–40, London, 1927

Smith, G. (ed.), *The Coronation of Elizabeth Wydeville Queen Consort of Edward IV on May 26th, 1465*, London, 1935

Wylie, J.H., *History of England under Henry the Fourth*, 4 vols., London, 1884–98

## USEFUL VISUAL SOURCES

**Note** Most of the journals of local archaeological societies contain articles on the monuments within their districts and these can be consulted for more detailed information on the relevant monuments (although the quality of the articles is very varied).

Avril, F., *Manuscript Painting at the Court of France. The Fourteenth Century (1310–1380)*, London, 1978

Clayton, M., *Catalogue of Rubbings of Brasses and Incised Slabs*, Victoria and Albert Museum, 2nd edition, London, 1968

Crossley, F.H., *English Church Monuments, 1150–1550*, London, 1921

Friedländer, M.J., *Early Netherlandish Painting*, 14 vols., Leyden and Brussels, 1967–76

Fryer, A.C., *Wooden Monumental Effigies in England and Wales*, London, 1924

Gardner, A., *Alabaster Tombs of the Pre-Reformation Period in England*, Cambridge, 1940

Greenhill, F.A., *Incised Effigial Slabs*, 2 vols., London, 1976

Longon, J., and Meiss, M., *Les Très Riches Heures du Duc de Berry*, London, 1969

Michel, E., *Catalogue raisonné des peintures du Moyen-Age, de la Renaissance et des temps modernes. Peintures flamandes du XVe et du XVIe siècle*, (Louvre), Paris, 1953

Routh, P.E., *Medieval Effigial Alabaster Tombs in Yorkshire*, Ipswich, 1976

Routh, P., and Knowles, R., *The Medieval Monuments of Harewood*, Wakefield Historical Publications, Wakefield, 1983.

Stephenson, M., *A List of Monumental Brasses in the British Isles*, London, 1926 (currently being revised by the Monumental Brass Society)

Sterling, C., and Adhémar, H., *Peintures Ecole Française, XIVe, XVe et XVIe siècles*, (Louvre), Paris, 1965

Stone, L., *Sculpture in Britain: The Middle Ages*, 2nd edition, Harmondsworth, 1972

Thomas, M., *The Golden Age: Manuscript Painting at the Time of Jean, Duc de Berry*, London, 1979

*Transactions of the Monumental Brass Society*, Cambridge, 1887–(in progress)

Unterkircher, F., *Le Livre du Cueur d'Amours Espris*, London, 1975

# *Glossary and Select Index*

**Note** This lists terms which are genuinely medieval, as well as terms which have been adopted since by convention; where a conventional term is included, this is made clear. The numbers of plates where particularly important or impressive examples of the terms can be seen are given in brackets. A general chronological survey of developments is given in the Introduction.

The spelling of Latin words is relatively stable, but that of medieval French and English words is extremely flexible, and readers should therefore be prepared to accept that the spelling in this list may not correspond precisely with that of words they may come across in their reading of other sources.

**Bourrelet** French term for a padded roll, initially found as part of female headdress, when the stuffing was dried plant stalks and other light-weight material, but later this feature is found in men's hoods and *chaperons*. From *'bourrer'*, to stuff. (49), (66), (80), (87), (90)

**Brassière** French term for a small bolero-like jacket, usually of black silk or velvet, worn under the *robe* by women from *c*.1485 onwards. (131)

**Caul** a decorated net used in the headdress of women of standing or wealth. In 'The Wife of Bath's Tale', Chaucer distinguishes between women who wear 'a coverchief (kerchief), or 'a calle', and in his *Treatise on the Astrolabe* (1391–2) he likens the claws(sic) of a spider to 'the werk of a womman's calle'. (51), (60)

**Chaperon** French term for a hood, of whatever shape, in the fourteenth and fifteenth centuries. Mainly worn by men, though various versions worn out of doors by women, particularly working class women. (20), (30), (56), (66)

**Chemise** French term for the linen undergarment worn by both sexes; the French, unlike the English, did not give this garment different names when worn by men and women. (87)

**Cloak** used in this book to describe all sleeveless garments of whatever length, which served as the outermost, protective layer of clothing. There was some distinction, absolutely clear at the time, between various types of cloaks and mantles, perhaps partly based on the size and formality of the garments, but it seems unnecessarily pompous here to call the cloaks of the ceremonial robes 'mantles' when the precise definition of the terms is unclear; the will of Lady Elizabeth de Burgh in 1355, however, talks of the three garments of her fifth and sixth best robes as *'cote, surcote et mantel'*.

**Coif** term generally used today, perhaps not entirely accurately, to describe a closely fitting cap, tied under the chin, and worn by judges and other dignitaries. Perhaps akin to the **voluper**. (4), (37)

**Cornette** French term for long pendent strips of material, like the English liripipe and tippet. Also apparently mid-fifteenth slang for a noose (François Villon). (20), (30)

**Cote** French term, sometimes used in English, for a garment worn over the *chemise* and under the *robe* of both sexes. Women's clearly laced up the centre front of the bodice, and had short sleeves to which false sleeves of more elaborate materials could be attached. Working class women could wear it as an outer layer on all but formal occasions, such as going to church, and in *The Canterbury Tales* the *cote* is seen as a fairly humble outer garment for men. It loses its importance in the male wardrobe by the end of the fourteenth century, but reappears looking like a tighter, inner *robe* in the last twenty years or so of the fifteenth century. (81)

**Cote hardie** apparently a garment for women which had the social acceptability of the *robe*, but the tight bodice of the *cote*, without its visible front lacing, and with full-length sleeves made of its own material. (17), (30)

**Cracows** men's shoes described in 1362 as having beaks (toes) a finger long, 'more like demons' nails than decorations of men'; attributed later to the arrival of Richard II's Bohemian queen, and by his day they had to be tied to the knee with gold or silver chains. Probably synonymous with French poulaines.

**Dagging/jaggs** serrated edges of clothing, at hem and cuffs of men's clothes, and cuffs only of women's clothes, created by use of specially shaped metal cutters, rather like pastry cutters.

Introduced in early 1340s; at its most lavish *c.*1380–*c.*1420; but continued in modified form to *c.*1440. (40), (56), (66), 74

**Doublet** a hip-length or waist-length garment with padded body, worn by men directly over their shirts. The hose were laced to it, sometimes under the 'skirt', and armour could be anchored to it by suitably placed laces. Term comes into use apparently shortly before the end of the fourteenth century; the garment may have displaced the paltok. In 1391 the future Henry IV had one of each made of red satin for use with armour.

**Ermine** the winter coat of a member of the weasel family, which turns completely white in winter, except for the tip of its tail; each black spot on white fur is supposed to be an ermine's tail, but the effect was frequently obtained by using scraps of black lambskin. In theory the use of ermine was limited to royalty, but many members of the aristocracy also wore it, or imitations of it. (111)

**Frontlet** the front section of a woman's headdress, introduced towards the end of the fifteenth century, and retained at the start of the next. Usually a band of black velvet, worn draped across the front of the head.

**Frouncing** (French, *froncer*, to gather) term used in 1340s, apparently to describe the gathering of the 'skirts' of men's garments. (19)

**Gown** garment for both sexes, apparently introduced *c.*1360. Term, though not the shape of the garment, continued in use thereafter to describe any formal outer, sleeved garment, regardless of its length and shape. Rendered in accounts in Latin as *toga*, and seems to be synonymous with French *houppelande* and then *robe*. (22), (35)

**Harlots** (also called gadlings, lorels: all terms mean idle, worthless fellows) men's *mi-parti* hose, worn laced to paltoks, in 1360s.

**Heuque** apparently a sleeveless garment, like a cloak, but slit up the sides to let the arms through. Worn mainly by men. (*74)

**Houppelande** Term introduced in France about same time as 'gown' in England, presumably to describe similar garment. Its most characteristic form is that adopted *c.*1380–*c.*1420, when it had very wide, hanging sleeves. The term is used in England in wills written in French within the period when it had this form, and the word seems to have become so closely associated with garments in that form, that when the fashion changed, the word could not survive a transition in connotation, which 'gown' did in English, and gradually fell into disuse. (40), (55), (66)

**Jacket** a garment in some way related to the doublet, and also to the jack, a cheap form of body armour which was a garment with metal plates sewn into it. The Fastolfe inventory of 1459 lists them under the Latin term '*tunice*', along with doublets, and they are mostly of velvet. The Norfolk Household Book, some twenty odd years later, has them as part of the outfits issued to men going to sea with Lord Howard, and implies that they had military uses.

**Kirtle** an inner garment, worn over the shirt or smock, but mainly worn by women. The term seems to replace 'tunic' about the turn of the fourteenth and fifteenth centuries, although the function of the garment, to provide an early form of corseting, does not seem to have altered. As an item of male dress it survived in the coronation robes and is mentioned at the coronation of Richard III. See also **cote**.

**Liripipe** long narrow strips of cloth hanging from men's hoods, and denounced for their narrowness in 1348 and for their length (to the heel) in 1362. Term seems to have been abandoned in favour of other contemporary term **tippet**.

**Mi-parti** (also **motley**) the practice of splitting a garment in two visually, having the right half in one colour or pattern, and the left half in another. This was particularly fashionable for entire wardrobes from *c.*1320 to *c.*1370, but remained in use for men's hose until at least the end of the century, and for liveries well into the next century.

**Miniver** the fur of the grey squirrel, arranged in shield-like rows, with the white belly fur forming the 'shield' within a narrow frame of grey. Reserved for the nobility partly because of the sheer numbers of skins required to line a garment: in 1406 the trousseau of the princess Philippa contained a gown made from two cloths of gold, worked with white flowers and lined with even more closely trimmed ('pured') miniver skins – for this 1300 squirrels had had to die, and she had other gowns just as lavish. (11), (37)

**Paltok** an as yet unidentified male garment, introduced in the 1360s and still being worn in the 1390s. Made of wool or silk and very short; used as anchorage for the hose. Those made for the future Henry IV in the 1390s were clearly meant to be seen, as they were embroidered with gold; this, combined with complaints about their disgusting shortness when they first appeared, suggests that, if not always worn as an outer garment, they could under certain circumstances be worn without over-garments, as doublets sometimes were.

**Pattens** wooden-soled shoes, with ridges under the heel and ball of the foot, to raise their wearer above the mud and filth of the streets, and to lessen the wear on leather soles.

**Pièce** French term for a small piece of cloth,

often of velvet or satin, worn across the chest for warmth or modesty; not required much before *c*.1450, when the *robes* of both sexes began to be worn rather open at the centre front chest. (\*96), (127)

**Pikes** See Cracows and Poulaines.

**Pokes** Apparently the name given indiscriminately to all the trailing sleeves of gowns *c*.1400. Etymologically, ought to mean just closed, bag-shaped sleeves, but these are far less common than the open-ended ones.

**Poulaines** French term for the beaked shoes worn by men in the 1360s. Prohibited in 1365 by Synod of Angers, and in 1366 Charles V forbade their use in Paris, and their manufacture and sale as shoes or hose.

**Pourpoint** French term for garment similar to doublet; word implies military links to 'points' used to tie on pieces of armour.

**Robe** (French; Latin *roba*) in fourteenth century means a suit of clothes for men or women; in 1361 the will of Humphrey de Bohun, Earl of Hereford and Essex, mentions *robes* of *cote* and *surcote*, to which he adds cloaks. Some people, however, regarded the cloak as part of the *robe*, and other garments, such as hoods, as additions. This sense of a suit of clothes is retained into the fifteenth century when a ceremonial outfit (which after all derives from the fourteenth century) is talked of. In everyday terms, however, from about 1430 *robe* comes to be the word used in France for the outer, sleeved garment of men and women.

**Shirt** term used in England for men's sleeved linen undergarment, as distinct from a woman's **smock**. Perhaps the distinction was felt to be necessary because a man's shirt would be shorter than a woman's smock.

**Smock** the female equivalent to the male shirt. Chaucer is careful to maintain the distinction, and in 1483 the will of Anthony, Earl Rivers, directed that his clothes and horse harness be sold to buy shirts and smocks for the poor.

**Stomacher** Conventional term for strip of cloth covering chest and abdomen; similar to French *pièce*.

**Supertunic** Anglicized version of word '*supertunica*' used in accounts kept in Latin in the fourteenth century. Probably all that is said about the *surcote* below applies to the supertunic.

**Surcote** French term, sometimes used in English, for the sleeved overgarment of both sexes in the fourteenth century. Women, however, by mid-century had developed a sleeveless form of it, with great, scooped-out 'armholes' which allowed the outline of their bodies to be seen from shoulder to hip, and it was in this form, the *surcote ouverte*, that the garment and its name survived into the fifteenth century. (6), (111)

**Tanné** (tanny, tawny) a shade of brown, perhaps with a slightly sandy tinge, which became extremely popular towards the end of the fifteenth century; at the start of the sixteenth century James IV of Scotland repeatedly clad his household in it.

**Tippet** longer-lived term than liripipe for narrow pendent strips attached to hoods and elbows of supertunics. Attacked when new in 1344 for their length. By the end of fifteenth century a totally necessary aid to allowing a man to remove his hat without having to lay it down somewhere or to carry it in his hand: the tippet, with the hat attached, was slung over the shoulder. (24), (31), (135)

**Tunic** (Latin *tunica*) a garment probably equivalent to the *cote*; the Fastolfe inventory of 1459 classes as *Tunice* jackets, jacks, doublets, petticotes (meaning unknown) and hose, showing that the basic sense of the word, by then at least, was that the garment was part of an intermediate layer of dress between the underclothes proper and the most formal and important outer layers.

**Voluper** seems to have been a fairly elaborately worked cap: Edward III had two worked with pearls and black silk ribbons in 1344, and one worked with pearls was repaired that year. Chaucer describes the carpenter's wife in 'The Miller's Tale' as having a white voluper whose tapes matched her collar, and she also had a broad silk fillet, worn high. Since this tale is set in Oxford, there is a chance that English dress, and not the dress of some foreign source for the tale, is being described.

**Wimple** used here, as it generally is, to describe the cloth which covers the chins of all women at the start of the fourteenth century, and is then gradually relegated to widows. In fact, how much of a woman's headdress was really involved in a wimple is not clear: Chaucer has his prioress in a pleated wimple, i.e. from the chin to the chest, but the Wife of Bath has 'coverchiefs' on her head and is 'Ywympled wel, and on hir heed a hat'. Thisbe he describes as hiding her face in a wimple, and Shame in the 'Romaunt of the Rose' has a veil instead of a wimple. It looks as though Chaucer's use of the word may be fairly arbitrary, and the solution to the problem may never be found. (3), (16), (120)